Through the Eyes of a Hawk

James Lowell Hawk

ISBN 978-1-64299-620-3 (paperback)
ISBN 978-1-64299-621-0 (hardcover)
ISBN 978-1-64299-622-7 (digital)

Christian Faith Publishing, Inc.
832 Park Avenue
Meadville, PA 16335
www.christianfaithpublishing.com

Printed in the United States of America

Chapter One

The Crash

We peeped behind the curtain, saw what some dead men have seen, and survived with it engraved forever on our memories.
—Ernest Gann, Fate Is the Hunter

I was sitting at home trying to piece my life back together. The previous week I was fired from my job of eight years, my dream job. Feeling the pain, shame, and fear overpowered my thinking. The company did give one-month severance pay, a tiny bone for my years of service and dedication to them.

The phone rang around ten o'clock. It was my old friend and "aviation guru," Safu Nana, asking if I wanted to come to his place and go flying. "Sure thing," I replied. I thought this was just what I needed for my mental health. Flying always put a smile on my face and rejuvenated my soul. Safu lived north of Chelsea, Michigan, with his wife, Judy. Their home was a beautifully remodeled one-hundred-plus-year-old farmhouse.

Their runway lay about 1,300 feet in length with trees on both ends. We pulled N5253X out into the sunshine. The Citabria was a pretty flying machine, revealing her sunburst paint scheme of blue and white and tail-wheel posture. After doing the preflight walk-around inspection checking fuel, oil, tires and making sure all control surfaces had full movement, we entered the plane. With Safu in the front and me in the back, we strapped in, adjusted our seats, and plugged in our headsets. The intercom allowed the crew to talk back and forth at a normal tone, much improved from the Beech 18 days when Safu and I communicated by hand signals and shouted back and forth. After start-up, we taxied down to the south end of the runway to establish what direction takeoff would be the most advantageous. Agreeing that south takeoff was appropriate, we reversed direction and taxied to the edge of the north end of the runway. We initiated our run-up, checking engine performance. With controls free and pedals free, we were ready to fly.

We could see Judy riding the lawn mower as we started our takeoff roll. As we accelerated down the runway, I gave her a wave. During takeoffs from here, it was imperative to break ground and establish a positive rate of climb right away as the trees come up quickly. Upon reaching flying speed, Safu pulled back on the stick, and we left the ground. I noticed the tail slipped to the left, a sensation I had never felt before. We cleared the trees at the end of the runway with room to spare.

We continued our climb, then without warning, the left wing violently rocketed up. The plane rolled to the right, heading instantly into the ground. Things happened so fast we never said a word. Time and distance froze. I'll never forget the sound of crashing through the trees and noted the unusual opening of the window next to me. Then I heard the loudest impact explosion I ever imagined. It went from a deafening rage to eerie quiet. My body bounced off the throttle control, bending the upper tubing of the airframe, and I landed against the back of Safu's seat.

Conscious but shocked, I started to regain my wits. I felt something running down my face. The back of Safu's seat and my light blue shirt were covered with blood that was still flowing from my face. I checked that my toes, feet, fingers, and hands were all working, then I called to Safu. He didn't answer. I called again—nothing. I was terrified. His head and arms were draped over the top of the instrument panel. I had to get us out of the aircraft now! Releasing

4

my lap belt, I worked my way to the door handle. I tried repeatedly to release the door, but it was jammed. Hearing little sounds, burbling coming from Safu, but no words, calmed me; he was breathing. If the door would not open, the only other way out was the window on my left side. As we had crashed through the trees, I remembered thinking what a strange time for the window to open. I grabbed the window handle. It was not a large window, but it was my way out.

My escape went fairly smoothly, except for standing in water and muck with fallen tree limbs all around. Looking into the aircraft, I noticed a fuel leak coming from the line connecting the two fuel tanks. Above the windshield a steady drip landed on the front panel in front of Safu. I had to move him now. We were not going to burn to death after what we just went through. Safu was starting to come around. I reached into the plane and undid his lap belt, grabbed him around the waist, and tried to pull him through the window. Safu was not a big guy, but having him folded over, he wouldn't fit through. I had to push him down below the panel by the rudder pedals and grab him under the armpits to pull him out flat. He was telling me how bad his leg hurt. The only thing I could say at that point was "I can't worry about your leg now. I need to get you out of here." The second position worked, and he was out. I got a look at his foot that was just dangling from his leg. It was a mess, and he had a wide gash on his chin too.

Standing in the muck where fuel was leaking, I knew we had to get away from the plane immediately. Acting as a crutch for Safu, we started to walk through the mud and branches. With difficulty, we finally reached a point on high ground where I felt we were safe and could stop. If the plane blew up, adrenaline could carry us further. I helped Safu sit down and tried to make him as comfortable as possible. We sat in the woods on this beautiful, blue-sky day. Catching my breath and winding down, I began to feel safe.

Safu began to ask questions he could have answered himself but didn't. His first questions were "Where are we, and how did we get here?" He looked at me with such a sincere stare I was scared he must have some kind of brain damage. I answered him truthfully, "We crashed in your airplane, and someplace south of your house, I think." The questions continued. I tried to change the subject with small talk, but the same questions kept coming. Then the question "Where is my airplane?" I knew this would be coming, and I did not want him to see his badly broken Citabria. I changed the subject, and again he asked, "Where is my airplane?" I tried to avoid the answer until he finally got my goat, and I said, "If you want to see your airplane, I'll show you." I turned him about ninety degrees so he could have a full view of the scene, then came the sadness. "My poor airplane. What will I do? My poor airplane." It didn't take long for him to see enough. I assured him that her last landing was completed and she did well. She'd saved our lives.

The ELT (emergency locator transmitter) was sounding its audio signal. This radio activates when an aircraft goes down. All aircraft in the United States are required to have this radio on board and in working condition. On impact, it sends out a radio signal on a certain frequency that alerts other aircraft to the position of the downed aircraft. The deafening audio from the radio marks the position for rescue. I told Safu that I was going to walk back to the airplane. I would try to silence the ELT. Back at the plane, I realized the entire electrical panel was still on. Nothing had been turned off. In our rush to vacate the crash scene, I missed it. I began to turn off the toggle switches one by one. To my amazement, when I hit the master switch, the ELT went silent. It was a huge relief. The radio was still sending out the radio signal, but the speaker was turned off. I grabbed my seat pad from the rear seat and returned to the bivouac. I positioned the seat pad under Safu's leg. Things were much calmer without the ELT shrieking at us. We talked about the weather and the birds that were flying in and out of the thickets around us. He paused, looked at me, then said, "You look like hell." I laughed and replied, "If I look like hell, what do you think you look like?" We knew we would be rescued, but when? Safu was doing so well, considering his condition. I had enough sense not to leave to find help, so we stayed put and enjoyed the sun. Time was suspended in place and couldn't be judged.

last landing N5253X

Chapter Two

The Rescue

Hope is the expectation that something outside of ourselves, something or someone external, is going to come to our rescue and we will live happily ever after.

—Dr. Robert Anthony

While lying there, I heard a voice calling out. I jumped up and started to yell, "Over here! Over here!" I heard movement through the bushes, then I saw Judy, Safu's wife. I ran to her and hugged her as tears ran down my face. I gave her my evaluation of our condition, reassuring her of our relative safety. I told her Safu had a broken ankle, a cut on his chin, and lots of bruises. The cut on my face had stopped bleeding. I said, "Please hurry back and get some help. We'll be okay." As quickly as she came, she vanished. This really uplifted us. Judy knew our position, and help would be on the way. We continued lying on our spot, making small talk, enjoying the sun, and waiting for our rescue.

After some time, we heard sirens in the distance. We wondered if this was our rescue, but as more time passed and with more sirens, I thought that maybe there was a car wreck somewhere. Then once again I heard voices in the distance. I jumped up and began yelling, "Over here, this way!" I stopped and listened. The next voice was coming from a different direction, away from us. I yelled out, "You're going the wrong way. Come back toward us." Finally, I could hear them heading in our direction. Two uniformed firemen/first responders appeared. It was a wonderful feeling to have help there and more on the way. I directed them to Safu and told them of his injuries. I started to walk away from the area and noticed a guy tailing me. Being a fair distance from the crash scene and Safu being taken care of, I thought now was a good time for a smoke. As soon as I pulled a cigarette out of my pocket, my "tail" ran up and told me I couldn't smoke. I said, "Yes, I can." He pleaded with me, saying that he would get in trouble if I smoked and asked me again not to. I put the cigarette back in the pack. The rescuer working on Safu handed the other worker a neck brace and told him to put it on me. Against my better judgment, I complied. But as he attached it, I began to feel real pain around my chest and neck. His partner told him he had the brace upside down. Once corrected, it felt much better.

More people began to arrive on scene. A couple of firemen were working to stop the fuel leak, and a helicopter was inspecting for a place to land. My next challenge came when I was told I'd have to get on a stretcher and be carried out. That's where I drew the line and told them that I would be walking out and there would be no compromise. They tried to tell me how important it was for me to be carried out, but I stood my ground. It's hard to explain my feelings, but after going through the crash, exiting the aircraft, removing Safu, finding a safe area, addressing Safu's wounds, and the fact that I was still standing, I was going to walk out. It was a driving force in my mind, and I had to do this for my mental health.

As fate would have it, while we were still deliberating how I would be leaving the crash site, a doctor and nurse from the helicopter came walking through the bush. The doctor began asking me my name and so on, while checking my back and neck. He looked at the two attendants and told them I could walk out, as per his approval. I felt great! The doctor must have known the importance to a crash victim's well-being to use their available resources.

Safu was now loaded in an aircraft litter, and the doctor, nurse, and firefighters hauled Safu up the hill to the helicopter. I asked which way was out. They pointed, and I led the way. The terrain was hilly and wooded but had good footing. I stopped to catch my breath, knowing that sooner or later we would find civilization. Then, there it was. We came out of the woods and into a field. I could not believe my eyes! There was more emergency equipment in one place than I have seen in my entire life. Fire trucks, police cars, ambulances, you name it! I found out later the crash happened at the point where three counties met, and all three counties responded. Someone emerged from an ambulance and motioned to me. With the help of the attendant, I climbed into the ambulance and laid down on the stretcher. She asked questions and checked my vital signs. I sensed she knew her business. She had that professional demeanor. My blood pressure was 250 over 150! While we traveled down bumpy country back roads, the nurse installed an IV as she hung on to a grab rail. I asked her how long she had been doing this job, and she told me eighteen years. Her full-time job was as a nurse at U of M Hospital, and she did this job for fun, something different.

I was sure that Safu was at the hospital by now. We made our way from county roads to city streets and finally to St. Joseph Mercy Hospital in Ann Arbor. It was a bizarre feeling as we rolled down the halls with all the staff staring at me. I was sure the word must have traveled fast that plane crash survivors were coming in. My face and light-colored shirt all covered in blood added to the stares. They took me into an examining room, and the staff began cutting my clothes off. They examined my head and cleaned my face while probing with lots of questions. They were very thorough. The doctor said there were no broken bones, just a cut under my nose and my lip needed to be stitched up. It took some time to get my nose ready for stitching as the blood was so deeply dried and the wound needed to be cleaned. I was anesthetized, and four small stitches closed the wound.

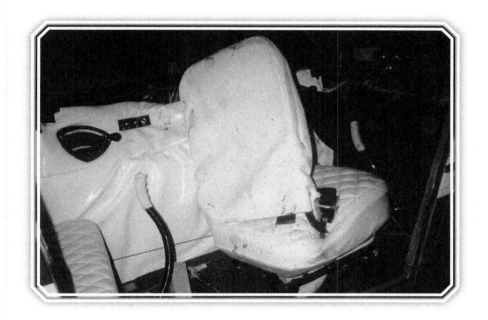

Chapter Three

Heading Home

Flying is not dangerous, crashing is dangerous.
—Anonymous

The next high came when my wife, Connie, and my daughter, Laura, were at my door. They came to my side, and we hugged and kissed, and I could see from their faces that anxiety had seized their emotions. The thought of never being together again really drew us closer. My doctor came into the room with instructions for my release. He said to me, "Tomorrow you're going to feel like you have been hit by a freight train." He prescribed a painkiller, and a nurse brought me a brand-new set of scrubs. Connie helped me get into them. The nurse reviewed my discharge papers, and we were ready to roll.

Before we left the hospital, I had to see my buddy, Safu. As I walked in, he was getting prepped for surgery. His battered body had not changed. I grabbed his hand, gave him a hug, and told him I would be back soon. Giving him one last smile, we headed down the hall, the aide pushing my wheelchair, with Connie and Laura at my side. As we passed the visitor lounge, Laura stopped and said, "Dad, you're on TV." I looked and saw a news report showing the crash site from a helicopter camera. It seemed surreal. News does travel fast. I had not grasped what a plane crash does for the local news.

We loaded in the car and headed for home, stopping to pick up my pain prescription. The shock was under control, and I was home with my family. We talked and had a bite to eat before I went to bed. The emotions created from this experience were immense. What if we had landed on ground and not in the swamp? What if the fuel leak caused a fire and we burned up before getting out? Those and many other thoughts would be with us in the days ahead.

In bed, I reflected once again on my life, and the calm feeling of knowing God was with us. There is only one thing that controls events like this. It is God. I prayed, thanking Him for blessing us and not taking us home with Him that day. I learned there is only one God, because on board the plane that day was a Christian and a Muslim. I prayed and gave thanks.

The doctor's prediction was on the money. When I woke up, I could hardly move. It took all my strength to reach the recliner chair in the living room. My face and arms were swollen, distorting my appearance. A bruise two inches wide from one hip to the other emerged around my waist, making it look like I still had my seat belt on. Connie's boss gave her the rest of the week off, and we sat and talked and drank some coffee. This was a treat we weren't used to on a workday. Thankfully, the pain pills were working as family and friends began arriving at the house: my sister Janet and her kids, Lauren and Christopher; my mom; my brothers Tom and Bryce; and my nephew David. My brother Tom nicknamed me Lucky Hawk. Someone went for lunch, and we all had sub sandwiches. This was my first real food since the crash and it tasted so good. All the excitement had made me tired, and as people left, I settled into a nap.

Connie had been in contact with Judy, Safu's wife, and she said that his surgery went fine. His ankle was reconstructed with plates and screws, and he would walk again. I also found out how Judy rescued us from the crash site. On the takeoff roll, Judy and I waved to each other. Apparently she stopped the lawn mower to watch our takeoff. We would always circle around and make a low pass by the house and then head out. This time there was no low pass, and she couldn't hear the airplane engine, so she feared we might have gone down. She started moving in the direction she thought we could be and found us, fortunately. From where she and I found each other, she wasn't able to see Safu, so she took my assessment and ran off to sound the alarm and bring help. She is one smart, calm, and collected lady. When all the newspeople started arriving at their house, she never gave out my name for fear my family might hear the news on television and not from a family member. I was sincerely grateful to her for that.

Day two at home started with the idea to go up north to our newly built home in East Tawas. I envisioned the therapeutic feeling of lying in our spa tub with a hundred-degree water. I ran the idea past Connie, and with a bit of reassurance that I was up for the trip, we went even knowing the three-hour drive would be trying for me. We also needed to stop by the hospital and see Safu. I already had his birthday present, although July was his birthday. I figured we both would celebrate a new birthday, June 4, 1997. We loaded the car and headed to our first stop, St. Joseph Mercy Hospital. Finding his room, we entered to see his leg in a cast, neck and head bruises that were much darker and swollen than the day of the crash. He asked us if we had a camera to document his odd appearance. I did take a couple of shots of him, and he was content. Then I pulled out his birthday present and told him my theory on celebrating the same birthday from now on. He was in agreement and opened his gift, a die-cast Beech 18 model like the one we flew together at Bentley Flight Service. We said our goodbyes and promised that we would meet up soon. Connie and I continued our trip to East Tawas though it was rough. The tub was wonderful and our time together in peace and quiet both relaxing and refreshing.

We arrived back in Livonia a few days later, and Connie returned to work. I remained at home, healing. During the next couple of days, large dark bruises began to appear on my lower legs and ankles. I called my flight doctor, Don Ross, and was in his office that after-noon. He examined me and said I had blood clots forming from the trauma to my upper body. He explained that clots form at the lowest part of the body such as ankles and lower legs. He put me on a blood thinner and instructed me to watch for any bruise movement upward in my legs. Call him if there were any changes.

The crash investigation began. The FAA completed their investigation and apparently didn't need to interview me. The insurance adjuster, a seasoned and experienced investigator, did interview me. He'd been involved in hundreds of accident investigations and confirmed what we all thought: if we had hit ground and not the swamp, we would not have survived. He explained that his company would pay for any medical expenses I incurred. He questioned me in a way that he seemed to be checking me out as a possible lawsuit. I came right out and told him that I had no intention of suing anyone, I was just happy to be alive. As long as my medical expenses were covered, I would be good. I could tell the relief in his voice. I had been told that someone who survived an experience like mine could easily settle for tens of thousands of dollars out of court, but I was fine with our agreement. At times, I think it would have been nice to get some free money, but the gift of life is far more important than lawsuits and money.

Lessons from that day: life can be over in an instant. Nobody knows when that instant will be. I've never worried about losing a job again. I cherish every day to its fullest. Don't hold back. They're precious, fragile gifts. Faith is the only answer to fate.

> *Oh! I have slipped the surly bonds of earth and*
> *danced the skies on laughter-silvered wings;*
> *Sunward I've climbed, and joined the tumbling*
> *mirth of sun-split clouds*
> *And done a hundred things you have not dreamed*
> *of—*
> *Wheeled and soared and swung high in the sunlit*
> *silence.*
> *Hovering there I've chased the shouting wind along,*
> *And flung my eager craft through footless halls of air.*
> *Up, up the long delirious, burning blue,*
> *I've topped the windswept heights with easy grace*
> *Where never lark or even eagle flew.*

JAMES LOWELL HAWK

And while with silent lifting mind I've trod
The high untrespassed sanctity of space,
Put out my hand and touched the Face of God.

"High Flight" by Pilot Officer Gillespie Magee
Junior No. 412 Squadron RCAF, killed on
December 11, 1941

Safu home from the hospital

proud pilots, beautiful Citabria

the runway

Chapter Four

Time to Fly

Real flight and dreams of flight go together. Both are part of the same movement. Not A before B, but all together.
—Thomas Pynchon, *Gravity's Rainbow*

My first infatuation with airplanes came early, around nine years old. My dad's job with Ford Motor Company had him on the road a lot. Mom drove him to the airport on Mondays and picked him up on Fridays. Needless to say, I went with Mom whenever I could. In my young mind I could not figure out how those big heavy airplanes could ever get off the ground. I was in awe to see them lift off the ground and climb into the sky. This was the era of the DC-3s, DC-6s and, DC-7s, still the props and pistons time.

One Friday Mom and I were at the gate waiting for Dad. He got off the plane and said, "Stay here by the rail. Someone special is on the plane with me." Because of the amount of traveling and the boredom generally associated with it, Dad felt this was a unique flight. As we stood watching people deplane, Dad told us that the special passenger was Dick the Bruiser. My mind immediately flashed to Big Time Wrestling with Lord Layton and watching Dick the Bruiser throw, kick, and punch all of his opponents with a look that showed he loved every minute of it. I had no problem visualizing who I was looking for. Then he emerged from the plane. The only thing missing from the vision I'd created was his wrestling trunks. Instead, he was wearing a sport coat and Ban-Lon shirt, probably because he couldn't get a dress shirt big enough to fit his neck. Things really started getting sticky for me when Dad turned to me with paper and pen in hand and said, "Go up and get his autograph, Jim." My heart was in my throat! I said, "That's okay, Dad, I don't really need it," but he persisted. My fear didn't change, but with Dad's perseverance and after he promised there was nothing to be afraid of, only then did I agree to go. As I walked toward this massive hulk of a man, not a single hair on his head, I repeatedly looked back at my dad to make sure reinforcements were at the ready. By the time I reached this huge man, my fear factor was off the charts. I stood in front of the wrestler and looked up with my big baby blues and said, "Mr. Bruiser, could I have your autograph, please?" He looked down at me, raised his hand, and patted me on the head and said, "I don't give autographs, son." Returning to my parents, I told Dad the mission was accomplished but not successfully.

On the way home from the airport, I was thinking of my Uncle Chuck, my mom's brother who would come visit our house about once a month. After he conversed with everyone, he would look at me and say, "Do you want to go for a ride in the car?" My answer was always "Yes," because it almost always meant a trip to Detroit Metro Airport to watch the planes. He would take me to the terminal building up on the roof where the observation deck was. We could get a good view of the taxiways, runways, airliners on the ramp, and the people boarding with the ground crews servicing the planes and all the activity. The highlight was a small yellow box that I could put a dime into and listen to radio transmissions between the control tower and the pilots. I had so much fun forming my foundation and love of aviation.

Our home was on the approach into Detroit Metro Airport. When the runways in use were heading into the south-southwest (21L and 21R), I would watch the traffic routed to the active runways. I became pretty good at recognizing the different aircraft and airlines. I also learned to observe the traffic that was going into Willow Run Airport. When using runways at Willow Run (23R and 23), they also passed close to our house. Back then there were still passenger airlines operating out of Willow Run.

There was another aviation place in my young life. That was in our basement behind the staircase. My parents had a root cellar where they kept canned goods and other things on shelves. One day while I was in there, I got an idea. Opposite the shelves were the back side of the stairs. Using some pencils, I started to draw my cockpit on the backs of the steps. I didn't really know what real aircraft instruments looked like, but I was using my imagination. In my mind I was ready for takeoff. I spent lots of time down there, starting engines, taxiing for takeoff, and flying wherever I wanted to go, to places as close as Detroit Metro and as far away as the North Pole. My map was endless, structured only by my imagination.

It was my love of airplanes that determined my Christmas wishes. On the toy market that year was a Steve Cannon pilot helmet that I wanted. This was from a TV show where Steve Cannon was the jet pilot. My brother Tom and I were crawling around in the basement one day, and we uncovered our hidden Christmas presents, Steve Cannon helmets. We felt bad about finding them; however, we acted surprised when we received them on Christmas morning. They were great! They had a visor and oxygen mask with a microphone inside. The helmet gave more realism to the stairway airplane.

My interest in flying the stairs began to fade. I needed something more realistic. I bugged my parents regularly to fly in a real airplane. I was persistent, and eventually my parents created a plan. They coordinated this with my Uncle Lowell and Aunt Carole who lived in Dayton, Ohio. The plan was for me to fly from Detroit to Dayton by myself. The family would drive down the following day, and I would return with them by car. I was so excited! When the day finally arrived, Dad drove me to Metro Airport, and we went to the Delta gate. Dad checked me in and walked me up the stairs into the airplane, a DC-7C. Dad, along with the stewardess, set me in a window seat toward the rear of the cabin. Dad told me to be good and that he would see me in Dayton tomorrow. The item that set the DC-7C apart from other DC-7s was that in the rear of the cabin, there was a circular lounge. That was real cool. The plane was not full for the trip. The pilots started the engines and began to taxi to the runway. Takeoff was fun. Rolling down the runway, I could feel the acceleration and then the wheels lifting off the ground, and then we were airborne. The stewardess was keeping a close eye on me and sat down a couple of times to chat. The view from the air was awesome. Cruising no more than ten thousand feet, I could see houses and buildings. I experienced what it was like to look down at earth and the feeling of being suspended in air unattached to earth. Before I knew, it we were preparing for landing in Dayton. The landing was smooth, and we taxied to our gate, where I saw my aunt and uncle waiting for me. The stewardess walked me down the stairs to meet them, and when she felt comfortable that I was with the right people, she headed back to the plane. My aunt and uncle recognized the value of my accomplishment. I felt thrilled completing my goal. I never forgot that first airplane trip, and my interests in airplanes never faded.

As I grew older my eyes were still always looking up. One Christmas I received a real aircraft radio. This allowed me to tune in to all the frequencies and listen to pilots and air traffic controllers. I learned the sequence of traffic into and out of the Detroit area. At that time, instrument approaches were being used. The Instrument Landing System (ILS) guided these aircraft to within two hundred feet and half mile visibility from the ground. When the weather was bad, I could tell by the tone of the voices that things were more serious. When the weather was clear, the radio chatter was more relaxed. Aircraft spotted the airport fifteen to twenty miles out, and the tower cleared them to land, advising the traffic to follow. I am still amazed at the precision and accuracy of flying.

Chapter Five

The Real Thing

When I'm up in the air, it's like I'm closer to Heaven;
I can't explain it.

—Jeffery Gagliano

The time was coming for me to learn to fly. I was fourteen years old, and I felt I was ready. My parents knew how much I wanted to learn to fly, so it came as no surprise to them when I started to push them on the subject. Dad told me he had a friend who owned a maintenance shop at Mettetal Airport in Plymouth, the closest airport to our home. Mettetal was a small community airport. My buddies and I used to ride our bikes there to watch planes come and go. It was a perfect bike trip.

Dad said we could go talk to his friend and get some input from him on flying lessons. I thought it was a good idea, so we did. I was surprised how much information we obtained from him. But not the information I wanted to hear. He explained that I had to be sixteen years old to solo in an airplane, by federal regulations. His suggestion was to hold off for another year and start training when I was around fifteen and a half years old. As much as that wasn't what I was hoping to hear, it made sense. He said I would just be wasting my money if I started now. Even at my young age, I could see the logic.

I continued to dream and save my money. For as slow as time seems to go when you're young, it went by reasonably fast. My first pilot lesson was on June 15, 1968. My instructor was Don Little, and my aircraft was a Cessna 150 N8095F. We flew out of Mettetal on my orientation flight consisting of straight and level flight, climbs, and glides. At the end of the flight, we went into Don's office for some basic ground school. My brand-new pilot's log was filled out by Don and signed. I had completed my first flight as a student pilot, and all was good. I scheduled to come back in one week. Since I still had no driver's license, one of my brothers needed to drive me to my lessons. I felt so good. I was living my dream.

I was working at the A&W drive-in by our house. I liked flipping burgers and pouring root beer and hanging with the carhops. My pay was $25 per week, and my flying lessons were $22, which included the aircraft, fuel, and instructor. I couldn't be happier! The flight lessons were pretty much weekly, weather permitting. After I demonstrated to Don that I could fly the plane straight and level and make turns without losing or gaining altitude, we started landings. All maneuvers are important, but it all comes down to landings. The pilot has to be able to get the plane down in once piece in all conditions. Don was tough on this. He had to be confident that I could do it on my own. We practiced landings during all lessons, crosswinds, short field, and soft field.

I was to the point where I felt confident to go solo. I knew that one of these lessons Don was going to say, "On the next landing, drop me off and you take it around the patch." That day came on September 6, 1968, in a Cessna 150 N23104. It happened just as I figured it would. Don and I took off, stayed in the pattern doing touch-and-goes. Touch-and-goes are used in training to save time and speed things up. Instead of landing, taxiing back and taking off, the pilot then lands, rolls out, applies power, and takes back off. During touch-and-goes, Don told me on the next landing to taxi over to the ramp and let him out. With the landing made, I taxied back to the ramp. The whole time Don was reviewing with me all the items I needed to remember. At the ramp, Don got out and said, "Have fun and I'll see you soon." So there I was, all by myself. I noticed right away how much more room I had. I taxied to the end of runway 18, reviewed the takeoff checklist, checked for traffic, and lined up on the centerline. I applied power while monitoring engine gauges and my runway alignment. Upon reaching flying speed, I pulled back on the wheel. I lifted off, and all looked good. Maintaining runway heading, I climbed out, turned left into the upwind position, all good. Flying the downwind leg, I checked the runway and the spot I was aiming for landing. Turning base leg, I reduced power and applied carburetor heat. Everything looked satisfactory. Turning on to final, I checked altitude and sink rate. Looking a bit high, I came back on the power and added twenty degrees of flap. With all things coming together, focusing on my landing spot, over the fence I came. Pulling back on the wheel. I started my flare, pulled off all power, and touched down—not real smooth but passable. I rolled out and taxied my way back to the end of the runway. I saw Don standing on the ramp watching me. I was nervous, but I had done it! Now I had to go back and do two more full-stop landings.

The biggest thing I noticed flying solo was how much more performance there was without Don in the cockpit. The plane climbed better and seemed to float longer on landing; I liked it. I completed my two landings and taxied back to the ramp. Don was there as I shut down and exited the plane. He shook my hand and gave me a big pat on the back. Completing my three solo landings granted me a student pilot's license. What a wonderful feeling of achievement.

Everyone had congratulations for me. It was just a great day. After everything settled down, I was struck with the realization that this was just the beginning of challenges and triumphs for me. Not bad for a sixteen-year-old kid. I was hooked more than ever by this flying joy.

I continued my training with Don out of Mettetal until September 1969. But I heard a former airline pilot was giving instruction in his own Cessna 150, out of Spencer Field in Wixom. I was looking for something more challenging in my training. My new instructor's name was Doug Wells, who had flown for United Airlines. He decided to leave the airline life and do something "normal." Instructing was a sideline for him after his regular forty-hour job.

Spencer Field was a grass strip with one north-south runway less than two thousand feet in length. It was located directly behind the Ford Wixom assembly plant. It is now gone, the airfield consumed by progress (like so many small airports today).

Our sessions started off great. We reviewed maneuvers, stalls, slow flight, and landings. Our next lesson we went for a short cross-country flight to Lansing, Flint, and return. I felt confident about solo cross-country flight and was hoping Doug felt the same. We made another cross-country to Toledo, Pontiac, and return. The flight went well. My radio work, pilotage, and radio navigation were satisfactory. Doug informed me the next flight would be solo. He wanted me to plan a trip from Spencer Field to Saginaw Tri-City, then to Mount Pleasant and return. He told me to be at the field at around 8:00 a.m. the next Saturday. He would review my paperwork, and then I would be off, weather permitting. When the day came, I was ready. I'd plotted the course and checked the radio frequencies. Doug reviewed my preparation and gave his okay. Flying in Doug's Cessna 150 N3693J, I did my pre-flight and buckled in. Takeoff was into the south. Climbing out, I began tracking my course to Saginaw. I used both radio and dead-reckoning navigation on this trip. Dead reckoning is the most basic of air navigation. It's done by drawing the route of flight onto the chart. Hash marks are made at prominent landmarks for checkpoints. From these, time, speed, and distance are used to calculate to the next point. It's very basic but can be accurate if done correctly. Radio navigation, or VOR, is incorporated with ground stations. The ground stations are shaped like an upside-down ice cream cone on a plate and usually found on or near airports. They send out a continuous signal in a 360-degree pattern. In the aircraft, the radio receiver is tuned to the chosen station by rotating a small knob until the needle is centered on the gauge. The "to-from" indicator shows your correct position, "to" if you're going to the station, "from" if you're going away from it. Keeping the needle centered will maintain the desired course.

I recognized Tri-City airport a good distance out; called the tower to receive my landing instructions. Flying into a relatively large airport with a control tower was a challenge. Completing the landing, I taxied to the transit parking then walked into the terminal. There I spotted a snack bar where a pretty girl about my age working, I ordered a Coke and asked if she would sign my logbook. She did sign it and it seemed that this was not her first logbook signing. I don't know if this is still in practice, but then a person signed the logbook at the field where the pilot landed, proof of landing at that location. Back to the airplane I taxied out to the active runway directed by ground control in the tower. At the end of the runway I was switched over to tower frequency and cleared for takeoff.

The flight to Mt. Pleasant was relatively short. I identified the airport a good distance out and began to organize my approach. With no tower at Mt. Pleasant I was on my own. I tuned in the Unicom frequency at the field and listened for traffic. I sighted one plane in the pattern doing touch–and-goes. I entered the traffic pattern forty-five degrees to the downwind leg, turned my base leg to final, making all the required radio calls. After landing I taxied to the ramp.

There's something about college town airports. They feel more alive, more active and have interesting people. This was the circumstance here at the home of Central Michigan University.

I purchased fuel and got my logbook signed by a nice lady behind the counter at the FBO (fixed base operator). Next was a quick walk-around inspection and back into the plane. I headed off to Wixom. The flight was uneventful and my navigation was on the mark. Weather was great that day and I know Doug knew it too. That was one of the reasons he let me go. I landed at Spencer Field and secured the plane. It was a great day for my first solo cross-country. I'd always done nicely on my dual cross-countries, but the first solo just validated to me that I could do it. I have always believed that planes are made to travel distances not just to fly around locally in circles. As time progressed I will truly understand that statement.

The following week I got a call from Doug. He said that I wouldn't be able to fly with him anymore. He and his friend had crashed his Cessna into the trees at the south end of Spencer field. They were both okay though they had to climb down out of the tree they hit. While they were okay physically, the plane was a total loss.

This was my first link with an airplane crash. Now I needed to consider where to go next.

I wanted another new flying experience, so I decided to look at flight school possibilities at Willow Run Airport. Willow Run is a large airport with a tower and large airplanes. Zantop Airlines was the big shot on the field. They operated DC-6s, Electras, and others. It was also the field that Henry Ford put together during WWII to build the B-24 bombers. He planned to build the bombers on an assembly line like the Model T. His contemporaries said it couldn't be done, but he proved them all wrong. Near the end of the war his factory was producing one B-24 bomber every fifty-five minutes, producing a total of over six thousand bombers. The first one rolled off the line on September 10, 1942, with production ending September 9, 1944. Only Henry Ford could have pulled off a task like that.

Willow Run airport holds a special place in my heart. My dad was an apprentice tool-and-die maker at Willow Run during the war. My dad's story is unique. He was from Rockford, Ohio a small farming town in southwest Ohio. After high school graduation Dad and a buddy decided to hitchhike to Detroit to find good paying jobs in the big city. As fate would have it they were picked up hitchhiking by a man heading to Detroit. When my dad told him that they were going to look for work there, the man gave them the phone number and address of a person to contact. When they arrived they settled into the YMCA in Ypsilanti and made arrangements to meet the man in need of workers. Going to the office building, they filled out paperwork and took several tests. Their paperwork was reviewed. Dad's buddy was hired that day, but my dad was told that he could not be hired because he was only seventeen and eighteen was the minimum age to work. He advised Dad that he would hold all his information until Dad turned eighteen.

Dad was less than a month from turning eighteen so he stayed at the YMCA and played basketball. On his eighteenth birthday he returned and was hired at Ford Motor Company as an apprentice tool-and-die maker at the Willow Run B-24 bomber plant. From then on Dad celebrated June 18 as his birthday and anniversary with Ford Motor Company. He retired after forty-seven years with Ford Motor Company. This had been his only adult job, something unheard of in today's world.

It was in this old terminal building I found a fine flight school. Scheduled airlines have been long gone from Willow Run. The school was McGrath Flying School, owned by Mr. McGrath, possessing a nice mix of Cessna aircraft. My first instructor at McGrath was Larry Hartsell who had all the ratings for instruction plus more. After we became comfortable with each other I started my cross-country flying again. We worked on ground reference maneuvers, steep turns, stalls and instrument flying "under the hood." This means positioning a helmet-like cover over the eyes to prevents the pilot from seeing the horizon. This simulates flying in clouds and using only the instruments for control. It's uncomfortable but it works for training.

I piloted flights from Mt. Pleasant to Tri-City and back, to Ypsilanti, Hillsdale, Toledo and return. Things were progressing okay. Then I got the news that Larry would no longer be my instructor. He accepted a job with the airlines. I couldn't blame him for moving on. I was getting close to my private license check ride and I didn't want to take any steps backwards. Luckily the school had a really good replacement for Larry.

I was introduced to Steve Wright, my new instructor and chief pilot. With Steve doing my training, I didn't miss a beat. With his background, I experienced some of my best flight training. Steve was a natural and a real people person. Every lesson we flew I learned more and more. At one point Steve asked me if I could come out the next evening about seven o'clock. He said he wanted to take me and another student on a field trip to Detroit City Airport flight service station and Detroit Metro Airport to visit the tower and radar rooms at Metro. I was excited and told him to count me in. The next evening the three of us left Willow Run for our first stop at City Airport. We swapped legs flying on the trip and I enjoyed some good night flying. The trip to the flight service station was excellent. I had talked to these people on the phone and radio but this time we saw them in person. While performing their jobs they were able to answer all our questions which was impressive. Our next leg of the trip was to Metro Airport. This was a very busy place. It serves as the main airport for Detroit, and it will be my first trip flying there. After getting in landing sequence with the rest of the Metro traffic, approach control handed us off to the tower for landing. Landing was fine but getting around on the ground taxiing at night to the FBO (fixed base operator) Page Airways proved demanding. Leaving the plane on Pages ramp they drove us to the terminal by car.

Then with a few phones calls by Steve we were in the tower. What an experience. We made sure that we did not interfere with the people working. Watching and learning how all this traffic is controlled was mind boggling! There was a lot of talking and moving about. The workers were great and answered our questions. Next we went to the radar room. The lighting was very low and there were positions with people seated at them watching all the tiny little shapes moving about on the radar screens. These workers handle all the instrument traffic IFR (instrument flight rules) and some VFR traffic (visual flight rules) into the Detroit airspace; not just the big airports but all the smaller ones too. All arriving and departing aircraft flying instruments are under their control. I was amazed at all the tiny blips or dashes on their radar screens, knowing that there were hundreds of people represented by the blips. I know the controllers don't think of it that way because the pressure would be too great. To help the controllers work load, they rotated to different positions every three hours within the radar room. After our tour was finished we thanked them all. I came away with the belief that these were special people with a special job that they do very well.

The Page Airways vehicle picked us up at the terminal and ushered us back to the ramp and our aircraft. We piled into the Cessna, working our way through the maze of taxi lights to the runway. The tower cleared us for takeoff and departure radar guided us back to Willow Run (a short hop). After a safe landing we parked and tied down the aircraft. There we said our goodbyes. Driving home all I could think about was what a great time this had been thanks to my instructor, Steve. This trip exposed me to night flying into high density airports and the inside operations of air traffic control and flight service stations. This night left me with a humbled and appreciative

feeling for the people who do these jobs. Whenever I file a flight
or talk on the radio to air traffic control, thoughts from that nigh
will be with me.

That flight experience convinced me that Steve was the perfect
instructor for me at that time of my training. He was a true professional flight instructor. He pulled all my training together and
put it into a final package. Showing me the areas of flying that were
important to me to pass my private pilot check ride. We both knew
it was close. On my next flight with Steve we reviewed all the maneuvers for my test and things went well.

Three weeks after our field trip, I was ready for my check ride.
Weather was good and winds were decent. I was introduced to Mr.
Stu Pete, a designated flight examiner for the FAA. Mr. Pete was not
an employee of the FAA, however he was given authority to administer flight exams on their behalf. I had some butterflies but my
confidence level was good. The test started out with the oral exam.
Mr. Pete and I went into a small classroom and he asked me questions on sectional charts and what all the designs and marks represented. Then he asked me questions from the Airman's Informational
Manual, a book published by the FAA that pertains to all aspects of
flying. I made it through that barrage too, then we were on to planning a cross-country flight with me and him. I used the same chart
from my oral. Mr. Pete asked me to plan a flight to Toledo, Jackson
and home. I had been to both airports so I felt confident and began
to plot the course, creating my checkpoints and doing all the time,
speed and distance calculations. Once completed, Mr. Pete reviewed
the plan and asked me more questions. After passing that hurdle he
then requested me to do the preflight check on Cessna 150, N60314.
Mr. Pete observed the preflight procedure and we entered the aircraft. I moved through the checklist, contacted ground control and
taxied out for takeoff. Mr. Pete informed me he wanted me to fly my
route to Toledo, and I responded with, "Yes, sir." We were airborne. I
picked up my course to Toledo following my checkpoints. We hadn't
traveled too far, and just past my second checkpoint he said to break
off to the right.

to the practice area and Mr. Pete asked me to per-
·ers. I did steep turns, slow flight, and turns about a
stalls. I completed the maneuvers with not much
·n he asked me to take us back to Willow Run. I
...re then he said, "Take us back to the ramp." At
ــoint I didn't know what to think. I believed I'd done acceptable work, but the more important question was, what did Mr. Pete
think? We parked at the ramp and went inside. I was on pins and
needles when Mr. Pete turned to me, put out his hand, shook mine,
and said, "Congratulations. You're a private pilot. I'll fill out your
temporary license, and by the way, you did a real nice job." That was
one of the greatest feelings ever! In the office we were met by Steve
and a few other instructors, and they all knew what I was feeling.
They congratulated me and were happy for me. Mr. Pete handed me
my temporary license with another handshake and good wishes. So
on the day before my eighteenth birthday I became a certified private
pilot. Wow, wow, wow! This was just the greatest. I had a wonderful
feeling in my heart on the way home. I had accomplished a big goal
in my life, and I was proud of it.

Chapter Six

Building Time

To put your life in danger from time to time....
Breeds a saneness in dealing with day to day
trivialities.
　　　　　—Dave English, *Slipping the Surly Bonds*

So what does a brand new pilot do on his eighteenth birthday? Call a friend and go flying. The first person to come to mind was Dave Mey. He had expressed an interest earlier on about flying with me once I was licensed. So now was the time I called him and he was ready to do it.

Off to Willow Run we went; checked out a Cessna 150 and to the flight line. Dave was the perfect first time passenger. His personality was very laid back and easy going, nothing seemed to shake Dave. I did the normal checks, picked up our takeoff clearance and we were airborne. Not really having a plan, I picked our school and our homes witch were easy to see. Seeing these notable places from the air was fun. It was a short flight but enjoyable. Dave had fun and I learned the feeling of responsibility. Having my first passenger under my care, we continued doing some fun flying. This helped me get relief from the regiment of flight instruction.

I took the time and money and checked out a Cessna 172, this has a bigger engine, two more seats, and more radios. This would work out well in my cross-country flying and take more passengers. The next level of training is to acquire my commercial pilot's license. This is really nothing more than building more flight time, cross-country and some added maneuvers. The next year or so was not extremely productive towards my commercial ticket. My spirit entered the doldrums. I did some flying and instruction, however I was not really regimented and funds were spotty. It was a low spot in my flying life.

As fate has its way of working into our lives, it struck again. I was reading the *Detroit News* Sunday paper and, as always, read the want ads aviation section. There it was, a pilot looking for three other pilots to share costs on a trip to Ft. Lauderdale, Florida in his Cessna 182. I called and Richard Matis introduced himself. In a very professional voice he began to explain the trip plan to me. He owns a Cessna 182 based at Detroit City airport. A businessman in town, he retains an airline transport rating (the highest pilot's license issued). He told me that he likes to do this trip once or twice a year. The cost of the trip was $200, price did not include meals or rooms. This was still a great deal and I told him to put my name on one of those seats. He was doing a shakedown flight the next day and he invited me to come. The other seats would be full.

From his directions I made my way to City Airport and to Dick's hangar. We made our introductions and pulled the 182 from its hangar. Dick was doing this for my benefit and the other pilots to get familiar with the 182. He gave us some final instructions before our final check. This is just what I needed to get back in the swing of flying.

The time came to be at the airport and ready to load. Dick had picked who would fly each leg of the trip. I was not picked first, so I was able to get comfortable in the back seat and enjoy the view. Dick flew from the right seat (instructor) and we all flew from the left (student pilot in command). Each leg was IFR flight plans, and none of us were IFR pilots, so this was excellent training for us all. The first stop on our journey would be Charleston, West Virginia, CRW. This airport was built around a group of mountains. The airport was constructed by removing the top of one of the mountains and building the airport on top of it, a very unusual setting. On our approach to the airport we flew on instruments. In and out of the overcast with some cloud tops displaying, the pilot made visual contact with the runway.

Sitting on a flattened mountain top and seeing mountains above me was unique, and something I'll always remember. After refueling and pit stops for the crew it was my turn behind the wheel, with the flight plan filed to Savannah, Georgia. The weather was to be instrument flying for a couple hundred miles with clouds breaking up then good visual flying into Savannah SAV. We were on our way. We did an instrument departure from CRW and one thing on takeoff that got my attention was the amount of right rudder pressure needed to compensate for the higher-horsepower engine in the 182. Flying on instruments in actual conditions was challenging. It takes practice and a trip like this was perfect training in the real world. This was not the average training flight of an hour. These legs can exceed three hours and required learning to pace myself and relax.

As forecasted, the weather in the Savannah area was pleasant and my leg of the trip was coming to a close. It was work and it was fun. Flying over Cape Canaveral and seeing its size and all the launch pads was impressive. The final leg to Ft. Lauderdale was clear and smooth, our goal was achieved, Detroit to Florida in one day. The only down side to this trip was the short time in Florida. One full day, that was the plan. We didn't have much time to enjoy the Florida weather. The time, while short-lived, sure was nice compared to Detroit in February.

Within twenty-four hours we loaded the plane, checked the weather, and filed our flight plan. After checking the weather Dick had an idea. There was a big weather system crossing the center of the country. His plan was to fly in a more westerly direction and in doing that we would miss the majority of the heavy weather. Taking advantage of the winds on the back side created a tail-wind condition. We were all in agreement on the route. Our first leg was from Ft. Lauderdale to Birmingham, Alabama, a change from our southbound trip.

Now it is my turn back in the saddle. With weather rechecked and our flight plan filed to Fort Wayne, Indiana, a long flight, we are hoping for those tail-winds that were predicted. Because of our flight changes and down time, daylight got away from us. I would be making our takeoff at night. Flying at night could be called instrument flying and added to that, changing weather was challenging. At our cruising altitude we were still on instruments while our rear seat crew slept. Dick and I were monitoring our ground speed looking closely for the boost from that tailwind. Finally, after about two hours it started to show in our ground speed, which boosted us to twenty-five knots. Total flight time this for leg was four-and-a -half hours, the longest flight of my career. This type of flying was new to me and a great learning tool. Landing at Fort Wayne, we changed crew for the final leg to Detroit City Airport. I crawled in the back seat and was so pumped up I could not sleep.

Dick Matis was truly a gift to everyone on this trip. His desire to organize trips like this training allowing pilots to get experience in these conditions would never be found in any flight school. His patience with three students who are non-instrument rated flying in instrument conditions was amazing. We all gained valuable experience on a long trip in a short time. His lesson plans are real world, equipment top notch, his character was right on and his personality outstanding.

This trip motivated and inspired me to get serious about my flying again, although weather was not favorable for flying at that time of the year on a regular basis. By April I was back at McGrath Flying School with a new instructor, Fred Ahles. Fred was attending college and he instructed me between classes. I was back to the practice area doing more maneuvers. Those negative feelings that the flying wasn't challenging again entered my head.

Florida trip arrival

fuel stop

Chapter Seven

Getting Serious

What's the difference between God and pilots? God doesn't think he is a pilot.
                                        —Dave English, *Slipping the Surly Bonds*

I knew that to finish my ratings I had to fly steadily and at a good school. I needed funding. My parents and I sat down together a couple days after my Florida trip and I laid out my plan. I showed them the difference between going to flight school in Florida verses staying home. They knew my love for flying and knew I was serious. $5,000 was the amount it would take to finish my ratings. My dad said he would get me the money the next day. I was so grateful to them. I now could see the finish line. This was the real deal. I was handed five grand by my dad as promised and told to use it wisely. I felt so good. My parents understood my need, were able to help and viewed me as an adult; all very important to me and my wellbeing.

Now with my educational flight funding covered, I began to lay out my plan. First, I decided to switch schools from Willow Run to Ann Arbor. Cessna Aircraft just came out with a professional pilot course and there was a Cessna dealer that was teaching it. The name of the school was Timoszyk Aviation named after the owner. The place was small, but equipped well. Jim the owner ran the maintenance side, the backbone of the business. Being in aviation maintenance for many years he had a chance to go on his own and he did it. His office manager, Angie Moore whom I have known for most of my aviation career, was also taking lessons. Their chief flight instructor and mine was Duane Morris, who holds all the ratings, has a good personality and not afraid to think out of the box. I explained to Jim and Duane my plan. I would give them $500 to purchase block time which included a discount. And as funds were depleted I'd replace them.

Another added bonus for me was the fact my friends Steve Demeter and John Watterson opened a Collision shop In Taylor. They named it S&J Collision. How appropriate. For two twenty-something kids, it was a big challenge and responsibility. Knowing I had a solid background in auto mechanics, they offered me a position with their company as an apprentice, assistant, goffer, and body man. The position fit me well and they were flexible with my hours. Adding income to my situation was of huge importance. Another lesson on how wonderful old friends are, the bond continues to this day.

The flight equipment was almost new, a Cessna 150, 172, and a Piper Aztec for multiengine training. The course included about four hours of programmed ground lessons for each hour of flying which were on cassettes and used a text flight manual. The beauty of the lessons was that I can do it at my own pace. My idea was to go Monday through Friday 8:00 a.m. to 1:00 p.m.; however, weather played a big part in this plan.

My instructor was great and I had plenty of resources. The only down side was the daily drive from Livonia. Flying with Duane was great. He knew my abilities, weaknesses and my desires. We made trips to the practice area and did more maneuvers. It wasn't long before Duane sensed I had a good handle on the maneuvers. Then he had me work on cross-country planning. Together we took a quick trip from Ann Arbor, Ypsilanti, Detroit, and returned. Duane signed me off for solo cross-country.

I was ready to get out on my own. Two days later I planned a trip from Ann Arbor, ARB to Toledo, Jackson and return. I asked my dear friend Steve Henderson to come along. The trip went well. We walked around each airport and had lunch in Jackson. Steve and I shared another good day together he liked the world of aviation as much as I did.

Our relationship began at Wilson School in kindergarten, 1957. Steve lived about five blocks behind me. Steve was the only class member that I shared the same classroom with from kindergarten through twelfth grade and we did all the sports together, too.

Shortly after the flight with Steve I shared a flight with Bruce Zikmund another friend from Wilson School elementary days. If Steve was my oldest friend Bruce had to be second. Our flight was just the local area and enjoying the scenery from the air. Bruce also enjoyed the view and the openness. Being able to discover the pleasure of flying with old friends seeing places we knew from childhood gave us all a new perspective. Now it's time to expand to more distant places.

Another friend from the old neighborhood, Galen Wolfe, who has moved to Minneapolis created an idea for me. Another friend, also from grade school, Steve Demeter showed interest in doing some distance flying.

One requirement for a commercial license is a long cross-country flight over 250 miles. I always thought that Minneapolis would be a great long cross-country trip. Steve Demeter would do the trip to Minneapolis. So we put it all together but could not find anyone else to go along, we had two open seats and no takers. That was not going to stop us. We made plans and Galen was looking forward to our visit. Cross-country trips are full of stories and this one I will always remember and I know my passenger will never forget.

The flight plan was set to go around Lake Michigan not across. I was trained never to fly over water in a single engine airplane farther than a safe gliding distance to shore. Steve and I departed Ann Arbor early on a Saturday morning. They predicted weather to be good with some possible lake effect around the Lake Michigan area.

Our first fuel stop was South Bend, Indiana and I checked the weather at the flight service station; all looked good. Off we went, working our way around the bottom of Lake Michigan. Visibility began to drop. I started a descent to maintain visual contact hoping it would improve. No such luck. Visibility was dropping fast. I was concerned about losing visibility completely and running into a tower somewhere.

I called Steve into action and handed him a sectional chart showing him how to look for towers and check their elevation. I was very concerned about towers. By now we were IFR with no forward or downward visibility and to top things off, I was not sure of our position. I'm sure my attitude worried Steve. I have never been in this predicament before and the pucker factor was high, but I did know what to do next.

I got on the radio and contacted South Bend radar and gave them our rough position. They told me to I-dent on our transponder which makes our position light up on his radar screen. By radio he responded to us, "Radar contact," requesting what our intensions were. I requested we would like to land at South Bend. Air Traffic Control (ATC) gave us our distance from the airport and a heading to it. Steve and I were relieved as we proceeded to the airport. The visibility improved and we were once again VFR. After landing I thanked God. We tied the airplane down and learned the weather had gone down around us. So we planned to get a room at the Holiday Inn, enjoy some food, a few drinks and make the most of it. And that is just what we did. Except for the drinks; enjoying a few too many. Our plan was to fly back to Ann Arbor the next morning, but the weather to the east was not in our favor. We were stuck. We didn't plan for a longer stay in South Bend. To make things worse, Steve had his final scuba diving test that night. We had to get home. I came up with a plan. We went to the North Central Airline ticket counter to find the time and cost of a flight to Detroit. We could get Steve home in time for his class. So we pooled all our money to buy one ticket. Arriving on time the Convair 580 Steve's plane, would have him home in less than an hour.

Here I am by myself with only a couple bucks left over. I had never spent a night in an airport before. This would be the first of many in my life.

When morning finally came, I checked the weather, and after defrosting the plane, it was clear sailing back to Ann Arbor as forecasted.

The flight back was somber, thinking how the best-laid plans can turn out so poorly in no time. I landed in Ann Arbor and taxied to the school ramp and shut down. In the office everyone gave me my space, which I needed. My flight instructor Duane asked me in a very subtle way when I wanted to get back on the schedule. I told him Tuesday. It was a humbling time on the learning curve but this is how we grow. Learning and appreciating that no one was hurt and nothing is broken, it all is good. Steve made his scuba diving test on time and passed.

The flying had been hit-or-miss due to weather, so I made good time pounding the books and getting ready to take my written test for my commercial pilot's license. I was working hard to pass on the first try, which would be a good ego boost and time-saver.

My choice for my next flight was Lansing, Kalamazoo, return. The weather looked great and I planned to do this one solo. Arriving at the airport I prepared a quick flight plan and filed it with the FAA. The weather was as forecasted with calm winds, great visibility and clear skies. I booked a Cessna 150 for this trip N52971. Climbing out, I picked up my course to Lansing LAN. While confirming my checkpoints and ground references I realized something was not adding up. There should be an expressway off my left side but it was off my right side. I tried to logically square this away. I became even more confused as time went on. I could only come to the conclusion that my compass was ninety degrees off. This had me very disoriented and I concluded it was time to find my way back to Ann Arbor. In my confused state, I was still able to find my way back and land the aircraft. After parking I headed into the office. Everyone had a confused look. I had planned to be gone for half the day. When I explained my compass went out, they were as confused almost as much as I was. The mechanics checked the aircraft and found nothing. I was asked if I had put anything metal by the compass; I responded no. Returning to the office with my flight instructor, Duane, we began an in-depth debriefing. Knowing now the aircraft was operating correctly, it was obvious the issue was with me. Trying to put an explanation to my dilemma, some facts were noted. In my mind I was looking for a certain expressway as a reference point and I had convinced myself that was the correct one. I convinced myself so well that I even concluded that my compass was wrong, by ninety degrees. A compass is the most reliable instrument in navigation known to man, when used properly. This was a lesson of all lessons for me. My mind was convinced that I was looking at the correct highway and I never questioned that thought. I was congratulated for one thing, that as confused as I was I kept my wits, stayed calm and found my way back to the airport. The conclusion was what I thought was an east-west highway in fact was a north-south highway and the most reliable instrument in the aircraft was showing just that, but I chose not to believe it. Look at all possibilities in decision-making. And last but not least, believe your instruments. As embarrassing as these lessons were, they made me a better pilot, and a better person. The following week, after this critical lesson I went to the Flight Standards Office at Willow Run Airport and sat for my commercial written exam and received a passing grade.

With my written test out of the way, a group of friends wanted to make a trip by plane to Chicago with me. Having all the knowledge from the past few trips absorbed in my brain, now would be a fine time to continue. I rounded up three friends and informed them we would go. The weekend after my written exam would be our departure date.

I did a complete briefing to the passengers and we were off. Weather was great and I always enjoy taking passengers when the visibility is excellent so they can get the full effects at six or seven thousand feet. Along the way around Lake Michigan we passed Ft. Wayne and Gary, names of past trips and thoughts of those trips still fresh. Our arrival airport in Chicago was Midway not the busy O'Hare which was still too busy for my level of training. I contacted Chicago approach control around sixty miles out and began to set up our arrival. I even produced a good landing for my friends and parked the airplane. With all that taken care of we called a cab and headed into town. Our plan was to have lunch at the John Hancock Building. Lunch was good and a couple of the guys had a few beers. I explained that was fine, however there's no toilet onboard the Cessna for the trip home.

We were now ready to travel up the elevator to the observation deck. I had never mentioned to anyone that I am very nervous in high buildings or bridges and have a fear of heights in those settings. So when the doors opened at the top we were looking out at Lake Michigan. My friends walked out to the windows and enjoyed the view. I was still in the elevator. They turned around and saw my plight and started to coax me out. They got a big laugh that the guy who flew our plane did not want to get out of the elevator. I finally did, but I was hugging the wall and never got next to the windows. We returned to the street level for some walking and sightseeing.

After a full day we headed back to the airport. When our cab arrived we all piled in and told him Midway Airport, Butler Aviation. None of us knew the area, so we counted on our driver to get us to our destination. Finally we made it to Midway and paid our inflated fair. We paid parking, landing and fuel bills and were cleared to go. I filed our flight plan, received taxi clearance and we were off to Ann Arbor, MI. Most of the crew nodded out. We made good time home, said goodbyes and all agreed we had a fun time.

The flight hours, cross-country flights and training lessons added up and were on track. One missing link was that long cross-country flight. I was itching to get this one in my logbook. I contacted my friend in Minneapolis, Galen Wolfe and scheduled a suitable time with him. The second attempt was set. I decided to do this trip solo. I booked the 172 for a long weekend and reviewed my flight plan. The day of the trip I was blessed with wonderful weather; winds were light and visibility suitable. Passing South Bend and Chicago put a smile on my face. Then came Madison and La Cross, WI. Approaching Minneapolis was a wonderful sight, a nicely laid out city and the Mississippi River added to the scene. This made for a perfect setting for the final leg of the trip.

I was ready to meet up with my old friend and best man to catch up on past times, have some beers and laughs. I parked the Skyhawk at Page Airways, instructed them to top off the tanks and park her for the weekend. As always, Galen and I enjoyed our time together. He took me to the First Street Station Restaurant along the Mississippi River with a relaxed neighborhood ambiance. After great food and a few more beers we walked along the river and checked out some trendy little shops. It always reassured me when we were together; it's like we were never apart. Our friendship never ends, even though it has been twenty years since we lived in the same city. The good Lord has truly blessed me with my old friends and for that I am eternally grateful. Most people are glad to say that they may have one or two true friends, but I can honestly say I have more than a half dozen best friends that have been part of my life for more than fifty years.

On my way home after a wonderful weekend with Galen I picked up a tailwind which is always good. The scenery of southern Wisconsin in early fall was picturesque with the trees beginning to show their brilliant colors. Completing my flight through Michigan and approaching the Detroit metro area, I finally completed my long cross-country flight.

Now the push was on. I know I am close to my commercial check ride, as does my instructor Duane. The mission now is to review all maneuvers, landings and have them down to perfection. When the flying felt right it was on to book review and regulations to reach the point where I was confident with my abilities in the air and on the ground. Duane signed my logbook meaning that I was competent for the commercial pilot exam.

I would be taking my exam with Paul Lambarth, a designee approved by the FAA to administer check rides on their behalf. Paul happens to run a small flight school at Ann Arbor near my flight school. Scheduling check rides with designees are simpler than with the FAA, however they have a reputation of being tough. Paul held true to those words. My oral and ground time took over two hours, including plotting a cross-country flight that we did fly the first leg of. He covered all maneuvers, doing a couple twice, then back to the airfield for takeoffs and landings, which went fine. Finally he told me to taxi back to the ramp and park it. Paul was a man of few words and never seemed to smile much. I was drained on the walk back to the hangar. I felt I did a good job, but there is always a fear of doubt with Paul. But he did issue me my temporary commercial license. What a feeling! All the time, work and money paid off. I can now say I'm a commercial pilot another step up the ladder to my goal completed.

me and Mom

me and dad

Chapter Eight

Push to Finish

Airspeed, altitude, or brains; you always need at least two.
—Dave English, *Slipping the Surly Bonds*

T he pursuit was on to the next level, instrument rating. This was the real challenge. This is the environment where all airlines, corporate and many general aviation aircraft operate. Everything will be new and foreign to me. As I have stated moving up from private pilot to commercial was mainly building time and adding some new maneuvers. Not so with the instrument rating, this is another world. The fear of learning all this new information was outweighed by the fact that this arena is where the professionals work and this allows aircraft and crews to operate as an all-weather environment. There will still be times when I don't go, stand down or fly to an alternate airport; all part of the training. I was eager to begin.

My training would all be in the 172 Skyhawk. Most of my flying would be under the hood, or in actual instrument weather conditions. The early phases of instrument training involved learning to control the airplane in climbs, descents, turns, holding a consistent heading direction, and altitude all under the hood (no reference to the horizon). The saying "Believe your instruments" is crucial; the technique taught is called the "scan." The process is simple in theory; observe two or three of the most important instruments involved in aircraft stability, spend a short time on each one, interpret their readings and then move on to the next. Observe all readings and make corrections to maintain flying the airplane straight and level. This exercise is done in a short time and sustains the pilot's altitude and course. Another term used is "mental gymnastics." With practice, it is amazing how close an aircraft can be controlled with no reference to the outside world. Training teaches pilots to scrutinize each instrument more closely than ever before, correcting the planes slightest movement.

Norm for the flight training business, I now have a new instructor, Tom Odell; Duane has moved on. Tom was closer to my age, had a nice personality, a veteran, and held all his ratings. As far as his flying skill, time will tell. My training schedule stayed the same; morning flying and ground school until early afternoon. Tom did not have a huge amount of flying experience but his training was fresh and current. He obtained his flight training on the GI bill.

Instrument flying was different in many ways. Just getting to the point of being comfortable and at ease in the cockpit took some time. VOR meaning (VHF omnidirectional range) tracking are the highways in the sky, the way aircraft move from point A to point B. Aircraft fly to and from VOR stations electronically connected by highways/airways.

Instrument landings are considered as precision and non-precision. The only precision approach is the ILS or Instrument Landing System. Basically this approach will guide the pilot to within a half-mile visibility and two hundred feet above the runway. These are called landing minimums. It is illegal to go below any minimums (altitude above the ground) on any approach. The non-precision are VOR, operate from a VOR station. The NDB, non-directional radio beacon operates from a low power AM band radio usually close to the airport. This system is the oldest system operating. The minimums are higher-roughly one thousand foot ceiling and one mile visibility, due to the fact they are not as precise and accurate as the ILS.

Training was moving along well; my ground school time required more time than flying by far and was just as demanding. I knew the written test was coming soon and I pushed hard to prepare. My level of confidence was increasing and my instructor, Tom gave me lots of valuable tutoring. I made the date at the FAA office at Willow Run for the test. A week after the test I got my results, I passed. Now concentration on the flying became top priority. Every training flight with Tom, he configured as though it were a checkride atmosphere. It was good and yet exhausting. Tom signed me off on my last progress checks, affirming my competence for my instrument check ride. Once again I met up with Mr. Paul Lambarth.

The process of revealing my knowledge started. His oral exam was almost three hours and he tried really hard to trip me up. Then we were out to the airplane with our flight plan filed. I began my instrument cross-country, picking up our clearance and initiating the flight. In a short time, we canceled the flight plan and headed to the practice area to demonstrate all the maneuvers in simulated IFR conditions. After completion we proceeded to Willow Run to demonstrate the approaches, takeoffs and landings. Finally, after almost four hours of flying Paul gave me the word to head back to Ann Arbor. Boy was I ready! Having flown this all under the hood, I was physically and emotionally drained. Back at Ann Arbor I was relieved to be done and he issued my temporary instrument rating. Of all my licenses this one means the most, knowing that a small percentage of pilots obtain this rating. It is a necessity to becoming a professional pilot. I was proud.

The last hurdle to complete my goal was the multi-engine rating. Flight training would be in the neighborhood of ten hours. Learning the complexity of a multi-engine aircraft is a challenge. Performing the maneuvers in the heavier twin was learning the feel and needing more muscle to move it around. Complexity is a big issue; as aircraft increase in size so does everything else. Instrument panels are bigger with added instruments. This means improvement in scanning the gauges. Having two propellers turning is a great comfort, however the most critical part of training is engine failure, and single engine operations. Having two turning is a good feeling, however when one quits it can cause real confusion. Engine-out training is performed at higher altitudes for safety. This procedure must be spot-on because rarely is there a second chance. To this day I still have the engine failure procedure embedded in my brain; (identify, verify, feather.) The sequence means, identify the engine that has failed, verify which engine is out, confirm, and last feather stopping the propeller rotation and aligning it in a position so as not to produce resistance or drag. This allows the air to flow cleanly through the blades not in their normal flat power producing position. Getting to that point quickly is critical for the survival of the aircraft. The pilot never knows at what point of flight this will happen but time is always of the essence. Something else I remember very well in training is the saying "Move fast slowly," pertaining to engine-out procedures. I can't tell you how many pilots and passengers are no longer of this world because the pilot, under extreme pressure, shut down the good running engine by mistake. It happens, and that is why pilots train regularly for this emergency.

The twin that I will be using in training, the Piper Aztec N5535Y, is a good trainer of middle weight with enough horsepower and weight to keep the training realistic. I really enjoyed flying the Aztec. Most of my flight lessons were created on unusual and emergency procedures. No flap landings, emergency landing gear extension, engine out, fuel transfer, cabin heater out and all the stalls, including landings and flight maneuvers. We also made time for some practice instrument approaches which were fun to do, but not a requirement of the multi-engine check ride. Training time was expeditious in the Aztec. Proceeding toward the official check ride.

Lance Gorden, the designee from across the field would administer my check ride. There were not many multi-engine examiners locally. No written test was required for the multi-engine rating, just an oral and flight test. The day for my check ride, I fortunately had good weather. I taxied to the east end of the airport where I met Lance and he began the oral phase of the test, about the aircraft and regulations. Then it was out to the Aztec for a complete preflight inspection with Lance asking me questions during the preflight. Climbing into the aircraft he informed me on how he wanted me to perform the flight. After takeoff we headed to the practice area and I performed all maneuvers he requested. Then it was back to Ann Arbor for takeoffs and landings. When Lance was satisfied, he directed me to park at the ramp at his office. There he issued my temporary certificate, my total multi-engine check ride flight time was one hour. In the office I received many congratulations from all the instructors and staff. This was the last license I was going to achieve for now. I was official. It was the fall of 1975, and I was ready to take on the flying profession. I even had a few dollars left in the bank. It was a good feeling. One thing I do know for sure is that without the help of my mom and dad this would never have materialized.

Chapter Nine

Classroom to Income

No one has ever collided with the sky.
—Dave English, *Slipping the Surly Bonds*

I had a lead on a job. It was through a friend of Cindy Carlson's dad. My friend, Bob Brincat dated Cindy all through high school and we chummed around. Cindy's dad worked for a company that owned a corporate aircraft. The plane was a Beechcraft King Air 90, a very popular corporate airplane. I was told that they may be looking for a co-pilot. I knew of this job opening about the time I started multi-engine training. I kept it to myself and I am glad I did because after completion of flight training the person in the job decided to stay. I *was disappointed* because it would have been a perfect job for me. Fresh out of training into a corporate King Air, though it was not to be.

During training I had a choice to make: to get my instrument rating or my instructors rating. I made my decision because I did not want to fly around the patch teaching new students. It just was not what I wanted to do then. Covering great distances and seeing the country was my dream. The down side was, if I had my Instructors ticket I could be working immediately. Fate has a way of sticking around.

Jim Timoszyk, the owner of the flight school I attended, knew my background in auto mechanics and body-and-paint work. He made me an offer to work in his hangar under the supervision of the mechanics, assisting in annual and hundred-hour inspections on aircraft. And when a charter came up I would be available to take it. Since I had no other offers, I accepted. Looking back, it was probably one of my better decisions.

The knowledge I acquired working in the shop was invaluable. The two mechanics I worked under were super and gave me lots of room, and I learned a lot. The charter flights were good too. We sold day rides. People came to the office with coupons from Cessna for a ten dollar intro-ride to promote aviation. Cessna would rebate the school to help defray costs. I wasn't flying as much as I would like, but flying. The intro rides with people experiencing a first airplane ride were fun.

Learning about the mechanics of aircraft intrigued me and gave me an insight into airplanes I never knew. I guess my boss wanted to test my abilities in painting and I took on a complete paint job of a Cessna 170 tail dragger. It's a big job. In the hangar we cleaned out a corner and hung tarps to enclose the area for a spray booth. I prepped and taped off all areas of the plane we did not want to paint. After it was all completed it looked really good and the customer was happy. Jim made good money on the job, and I was glad I had fun and now could say I painted an airplane.

One of my most memorable times working at the hangar occurred during an open house not quite an air show at Ann Arbor Airport. My job that day was to make sure the planes on display were in place and the planes being used for rides were positioned and ready for work. Booths were set up and a good crowd was on hand. I always enjoyed doing the rides. I've flown grandparents and grand-kids (my favorite), boyfriends and girlfriends and families. We were only allowed to fly them one trip around in the pattern. For most of them it was their first time in the air. At these times I remember why I learned to fly. Giving these people fifteen to twenty minutes in the air, flying around the patch, made me proud and warmed my soul. To bring them into the world of flying and knowing they were completely in my care, thrilled me.

Finishing off the day was something else. As the day was coming to an end, Jim, my boss wanted us to move the aircraft back to our hangar on the opposite end of the field. He told me to get into the new 150 on display and drive her home. This was a new trainer that Jim had just purchased a few months earlier. I entered the cockpit, read the check list and started the engine. Within seconds of engaging the starter I heard a tremendous noise and the aircraft began shaking violently. I thought the engine blew up. I pulled the engine-mixture control, to stop the engine. Exiting the aircraft I was shocked. There was another aircraft attached to mine. Its propeller had chopped into the tail section and part of the rear fuselage of my aircraft. It was a dreamlike scene. People started flooding to the area. Civil Air Patrol personnel began to set up a perimeter around the scene. My boss and other employees questioned the pilot of the plane that caused this mess. The aircraft was a Cessna 170, a tail dragger, meaning there is no nose gear like the 150. On the 170 Cessna the third wheel is under the tail and the nose sits up higher, not as good for taxiing visibility. The pilot, a female and an officer of the Civil Air Patrol was parked behind, and to the left of my aircraft. Having no idea what happened she just taxied out, did not make the turn and ran into me. Seems hard to believe. Had she made less of a turn she would have ended up inside the left rear of the wing and the door area where I was seated. That could have been another story. Once again fate intervenes in my life in aviation. The 150 was rebuilt in about three months. Recording serious damage for such a new aircraft was a shame.

Chapter Ten

Younger Years in Suburbia

*Whoever inquiries about our childhood wants to
know about our soul?*

—Erika Burkart

My Grandpa Schutt my mom's dad was a conductor for the New York Central Railroad. He was on a run to Chicago from Detroit. Not long after departing he was collecting tickets and getting the passengers settled in. He sat down to eat his lunch, but he never took a bite. The passengers thought he was napping. At fifty-eight years old, Grandpa died on a train to Chicago. His body was removed from the train in Kalamazoo, Michigan, and transported back to Detroit. My uncle Chuck, Grandpa's son worked in the stationmaster's office and took the call of Grandpa's passing.

I remember Chuck arriving to inform the family of the sad news. As Uncle Chuck told the story, in my four-year-old mind all I could envision was Grandpa's train going over a trestle bridge and the train falling off the tracks and crashing down. That must have been the only way my young mind could visualize death. The only other memory of Grandpa's death was riding in the big black limousine behind the hearse to the cemetery. The vehicles were huge. Now Grandpa is only memories, always smiling and happy.

Another memory I have was the day Grandpa Schutt took me to the New York Central Station in Detroit. It reminded me of a big castle from years ago with lots of stone work design. In the station with all the people and announcements of train departures and arrivals, the sound reverberated through the whole building. "Will Jim Hawk please report to the Station Manager's office?" I could not believe it. I was astonished and Grandpa looked at me and smiled.

After Grandpa's passing, Grandma sold the house in Detroit and moved to Livonia just a few blocks from our home.

Grandpa Hawk had passed away just a few months after Mom and Dad were married. He was only a memory from stories told, I feel I would have enjoyed his company. Though his life was short it was a full life. I was without a grandpa's influences from an early age, an enormous void in my life growing up.

Our home was at 9880 Harrison. Across the street from us was Wilson Elementary School and a city park, a great place for us to spend our play time and walk to school. I am the youngest son of three (little sister seven years younger than me, Janet). Bryce was the oldest, four years my senior and Tom in the middle two years ahead. Having two older brothers helped me a lot growing up. Very few times did I have problems with bullies or kids with attitudes. I was pretty much left alone. I remember my first day of school. Mom walked me up to the door and I felt very sad until the door opened. That was when I first met Steve Henderson, and started a friendship that lasted a lifetime. Steve and I were together in public school classes through twelfth grade. That friendship was special. We knew each other well, both in school and out, our friendship continued to grow.

Livonia was a wonderful place to live and grow up. It was growing fast and turning empty fields into subdivisions practically overnight. Schools were full and new ones constructed to meet the demand. Storm sewers, roads and streetlights followed after the subdivisions.

After supper, kids wanted to return playing outside. The common instructions from our parents were "Be sure you're home when the streetlights come on." In our younger years this was our evening time-piece. As we grew older, during the summer our time was mostly spent in the park across the street. It was a gathering place for all our friends. Just hanging out was the big thing. We didn't do a lot, just being together was good enough for us.

We rode our bikes to B&B Drugstore at the end of our street and Plymouth Rd. They had a soda fountain and candy counter. We loaded up on penny candies and maybe got a Cherry Coke (small six cents) or a cake roll sundae (twenty-one cents) then rode back to the park to hang out.

One of our favorite spots was the big oak in the rear of the park. This was the biggest tree in the park. We all had our favorite limb to sit on. We climbed up into the tree and just and talked telling stories and enjoying the view. We looked like a bunch of monkeys to anyone walking through the park. One day after a trip to B&B Drugs with candy and ice cream we bought, all of us climbed the big oak. One of our friends, Craig Gray bought an ice cream cone. He liked it but could not keep it down. This particular day another friend showed up, Kimble Lee who was not a regular in the park but wanted to join us in the tree. So he began to climb and as Kimble was moving up Craig vomited his semi-digested ice cream onto Kimble's head. Needless to say Kimble did not finish his climb but he had some choice words as he jumped on his bike and peddled away. We were all laughing so hard it is a wonder none of us didn't fall out of the big oak. That was not a nice thing to have done, but this is an example of how kids can be cruel to each other and harm feelings.

In the back of the park by the big oak there was a cleared area. We got the word the city was putting in a new piano slide in this spot. We didn't really know what a piano slide was, so we went to find out. It is about twenty-five feet long with a height at fifteen feet and it slopes down to about two feet on the opposite side making the angle look like a piano with a hand rail around the upper edge. This is all mounted into the ground at about a fifty degree angle. To play on it, kids get a running start and jump onto the face (the slide) and try to run up to the top.

Needless to say once installed and operational it drew lots of kids. Everyone was learning the technique on the new slide. It was fun, but caused the most emotional trauma of my young life by exposing parts of my body never seen before by strangers, let alone girls. I was using the slide and getting good at the way it worked. I made my run to the top of the slide and was hanging onto the top rail with my body stretched out down the slide. My problem started as I was lying on the slide at the top. One of my Brother Tom's friends, John Salvatore, a big boy to say the least, made his run up the slide. During his attempt to the top he could not make it. Lying on the slide John grabbed the rear of my jeans to hold on. My pants couldn't handle the pressure of John's weight and the angle of the slide. My pants tore off! I was hanging on in my underwear! I let go and slid down to the ground, running away from the crowd crying in extreme embarrassment. After redeeming some of my composure I walked home, thinking how much I hated John Salvatore, although he was forgiven only after some time. It's not fun every day to be Little Hawk.

I was always wanting to hang around with my brother Tom and his friends. I can't really say why, but I always seemed to be with them. This was something unacceptable to my brother, although his friends liked my company. I was given the nickname Little Hawk by them, which was fine with me. Tom, two years older, exposed me to things early on, like smoking cigarettes. Back then almost everyone smoked, and to be one of the guys I started around twelve years old. Even being an athlete I took up smoking. Nothing can hurt me was my thinking. I can do anything. On our regular trips to B&B Drugs, I would pick up a pack of Pall Malls or Lucky Strikes and a sixteen-ounce Pepsi for about fifty cents, take it back to the park that we called the "woods," and we were set.

Chapter Eleven

The Things Kids Find to Do

Children have never been very good at listening to their elders, but they have never failed to imitate them.

—James Baldwin

We spent a lot of time just sitting around with not a lot to do. So we would come up with some pretty strange thinking. One day someone had this great idea to climb the big slide (not the piano slide) with our bikes and ride them down. I wanted nothing to do with that, as my bike was too valuable to me. I needed it for my paper route and besides, that idea was nuts I thought. But there is always someone ready for the challenge. This time it was Mike McKeon. His bike was rough to start with and he didn't have a paper route so up he climbed carrying his bike. This slide was tall and by the time Mike reached the top he had a revelation that he could get killed riding down the slide. Those of us on the ground were giving him lots of advice, some good and some not so good. Finally Mike drew the conclusion that he was not riding the bike down and not carrying it down. His only other option was to put the empty bike on the slide and push it off. That was just what he did. When Mike had the bike in position he gave a little push and down it came gaining speed until about three quarters down it flipped off and hit the ground. Everyone was laughing. It was one of the classic moves from the boys in the woods always looking for something to pass the time. Needless to say Mike did not ride his bike home that day.

There were no girls that constantly hung around the woods with us. Some of the guy's sisters and a few girls from the neighborhood would stop by but they never stayed long. It was a boy's club with lots of smoking and spitting. Spitting was important to us. We would sip pop but instead of swallowing, spit it out between our front teeth to see who could shoot it the farthest. Boys do weird things.

With the same group we were hanging out by the big slide swinging on the swings. The city had fifty-five gallon drums, painted them green and distributed them throughout the park for garbage cans. There happened to be one close to the swings. Someone came up with the idea of getting me in the drum and the others would pour sand from the playground into the drum with me in it. Don't ask how I agreed to this, but I did. As I kneeled in the drum the sand began pouring in. I adjusted my body to make it feel more comfortable. I was told that they were only going to fill it half way. Boy what a sucker I was! My friends continued past my waist up to my neck. Little did I know once my feet and legs were covered I wasn't going anywhere. So here I am in this fifty-five gallon drum filled with sand and the only things showing are my head and neck. Needless to say they were having a great laugh on me. They weren't done yet, though. Someone thought it's time for a run to B&B Drugstore so everyone took off leaving me in the barrel, telling me they won't be long and laughing all the way out of the park. Here I am going nowhere stuck in this barrel. I saw two young kids walking up the path to the swings. They started to approach me and I figured they could spring me. I yelled to them, "Hey, come over here. I need your help!" They saw only my head in this barrel and looked confused as I asked them to push the barrel over. They tried, but it must have weighed hundreds of pounds. Now I started to get worked up over the mess I was in. Finally the group returned from B&B Drugs still laughing and having fun on me. They decided it was time for my release. They pushed the barrel over and dug me out. After that I'd had enough, so I called it a day and walked home.

One of the most unforgettable times took place in my own backyard in the spring. In those days it was commonplace to burn all burnable trash in a wire drum. I had been checked out by Dad to do this job and I liked it. It reminded me of camping and being around the camp fire. This day it was cold and windy. I gathered the burnable rubbish and headed to the back yard, I loaded up the wire basket and started the fire. It was cold so I stood close to the fire to find some warmth. In this process I looked down at my feet and saw my pant leg was on fire. Knowing the proper procedure for this predicament, I laid down and began to roll. One of the most important parts of this drill—I was either not told, or I did not remember—was to roll slowly. I was not. As I looked down at my leg the flames were much greater than when I first hit the ground. Panic hit me. For the first time in my young life I thought I was going to burn to death. I knew I had to act fast; rolling was not working. I looked for help. There was a low spot where snow and rain would form a rather big puddle. I rose to my feet and began a sprinter's run to our temporary pond, entering it headfirst. The wet and cold wasn't even noticed. The fire was out and I was not going to be burned alive. I took a breath and examined my right leg to find my pant leg was mostly missing, with some charred pieces sticking to my leg. It was a grayish color with a few darker spots. Now I had to pick myself up and go into the house and tell Mom. I sat down just inside the rear door on a chair for us kids to remove our boots and outdoor clothing. My right boot protected my ankle and foot, no damage there. As I was removing my clothes I called to Mom. She was preparing supper in the kitchen. "Don't get mad at me, but I burned my pants," I yelled to her. She dropped what she was doing, verbally giving me the shake down. And as she reached me her eyes spotted my leg. She let out a gasp and her complete attitude changed. She was panicking. To this point I was calmly in shock, but now all that changed. I started to cry and became scared. She told me we had to go to the hospital as she began looking for a pair of pants I could wear.

I slowly got my burned pants off and a new pair on, the baggiest pair I owned, my Cub Scout uniform pants. We began to head out the door and Dad surprised us. He showed up after work and took control. He picked me up and laid me in the back seat of the car, with mom in the front. Dad drove to St. Mary Hospital in Livonia. I'm put in an examining room and the doctor began assessing my leg. With a nurse they start removing burnt skin and parts of my charred pants from my leg. Then it was cleaned very well, ointment was applied and lots of gauze wrapped with an ace bandage. We were told not to do anything to it and to come back in three weeks to the office. There was some pain and discomfort. My folks were told to give me aspirin, which they did. Back then the best treatment for a burn was to keep it covered and not to let it be exposed to the air.

Back at school, telling everyone the story was not fun. The doctor did want some elevation to my leg, so an extra chair was placed next to me to use as needed. The worst part of this whole deal was that as burns are closing up and the healing process starts, they begin to stink and it was noticeable. In the morning before school I would cry, telling Mom I did not want to go to school because my leg stunk and everyone could smell it. She took me into her room, took out some perfume and sprayed it on my leg dressing. I did not think this would work, however no one complained after that. Mom's touch came through again.

The time came to revisit the doctor and remove my bandage. First the ace bandage, then the wrapped gauze and finally the gauze pads, which had been on so long they had become part of the scab. The nurse and doctor began to cover my leg with hydrogen-peroxide to loosen the scabs. My leg looked like a volcano erupting. However, it did some loosening, but mostly they pulled the pads off. I do remember pain and a lot of blood, but the pads came off. Each visit the bandages became smaller with less bleeding. The burns I sustained were mainly third degree with some of the edges second degree. I suffered no lasting effects from the burns just scarring. I continued with my Little League football career. This was quite an ordeal for a sixth grader. It taught me early on how fragile life is and how life can be snuffed out in an instance.

Another one of the group's fun spots in the area was the Detroit Race Course a big horse racing track. It was located about a half mile from home. We would walk past the railroad tracks or as we called them the "tracks." There was a tall security fence that we had to get over to enter the property. Most of the time we would go over the fence, or if we could find a low spot on the bottom we'd crawl under. Once inside the grounds we'd make our way to the track. On the back stretch we would lie on our bellies looking under the large white curtains covering the outside of the track. It was fun to watch the horses training and come real close to us. A couple of times we went at night when the real racing took place. This was different, to see twelve to fourteen horses on the track at once. Occasionally we'd get spotted by security and they would run us off. We got a thrill from the chase. One day one of us got the bonehead idea that it would be fun to climb the water tower used by trucks to wet down the track. There was a nozzle about four inches wide that the trucks used to load up the water then spread it around the track. One of the guys pulled the lever and the water came rushing down. We were never caught or even chased for that one, but a lot of water covered the ground.

In late fall the DRC brought motorcycle racing. We didn't have to watch under the fence this time. Dad bought tickets for us and we watched the racing from the stands. It was fun watching the racing on dirt. They were fast and aggressive. One year Dad had some heart issues and ended up in St. Mary Hospital. During the race that year there was a collision on the track. One driver was taken to the hospital and ended up, in Dad's room. It was very interesting listening to his stories for a young guy like me. Like many things in this country the DRC is gone.

Just down the tracks from the DRC was a small magnesium plant. This was a small factory that fabricated parts using magnesium. Machining produces lots of excess shavings that were discarded. Our plan was to go over the security fence. (For some reason no one ever explained to us what security fences were for, or we didn't listen). Once in the back lot we took as much of the shavings as we wanted, usually a small bag full. We had to be careful in the back lot located very close to the building to make sure there was no one inside. Our trips were usually later at night and weekends. Getting this magnesium fascinated us. It was tough to get burning but when it lit it burned white hot and bright, and also burned in water. Not much will put it out. As usual, it was something we shouldn't be playing with but we did, a common thread in our young lives, never with intent to hurt anyone.

As usual on one of our trips, one of my buddies got an idea to grab a five gallon bucket that was inside the lot, fill it with magnesium shavings then take it to an old abandon well. Once there, someone lit the bucket and dropped it down the well. I was not interested in this scheme. So a few of us began to walk away leaving the plant, and the others there. My group was about half way down the road when we heard this loud explosion and turned to see flames shooting above the trees. It was quite a sight and I'm glad I viewed it from a distance. Our first concern was our buddies. We stopped for a moment and before long they came running down the street, laughing, yelling and having a good time. When they caught up to us we found out everyone was okay and no one hurt. I'm glad that we did not spend a lot of time at the magnesium factory in our growing years. It was too dangerous.

Chapter Twelve

Wheels Broaden Our Exploration

*If you let yourself be absorbed completely, if you sur-
render completely to the moments as they pass, you
live more richly those moments.*
          —Anne Morrow Lindbergh

One of my biggest joys was bicycle riding. This was used first as transportation around the neighborhood and a necessity delivering newspapers. Bicycles opened our world, allowing travel far beyond what walking could take us and going places we never had been before. And by allowing us to create income hauling our newspapers it put cash in our pockets on a weekly basis. My main working bike was a Schwinn Deluxe Heavy duty. This was the work horse carrying my papers daily and any other job needed done. It was one of Schwinn's biggest sellers, built with heavy duty frame, big tires, comfortable saddle and a big spring on the front wheel to absorb shock and make for a smoother ride. It looked the part. However, my fun ride was a bike called a Stingray, also made by Schwinn. This machine looked its name. Built on a twenty-inch frame with high-way handlebars and a banana seat, it was sweet. The banana seat was built for two which allowed us to carry a passenger, hopefully a girl. The bikes were usually painted in bright colors; mine was yellow with a white seat. These bikes were extremely popular with us kids, and everyone had one. We loved to ride together as a group, never as a gang, just buddies. Riding down the street we loved to do one of our favorite move, the wheelie. This maneuver was done by pulling back on the handlebars, lifting up the front wheel and peddling just fast enough to keep the wheel off the pavement. The challenge was to see who could keep the front wheel off the pavement the longest. As we rode, we constantly challenged each other. Some had the technique down better than others, but we all had fun. Some of the guys went a step further and rode unicycles, something I never mastered and really didn't care to, I liked two wheels.

For me the real fun was going on trips, expeditions on bikes. A group of us would take off on field trails from our homes in the morning and head to Hines Park about three miles from our neighborhood. This park was our salvation for kids living in the city/suburbs. Hines Park followed the Rouge River, winding its way from northwest of Detroit through the suburbs and emptying into the Detroit River. This river basin made a natural drainage area for the western suburbs, saving many homes from potential flooding. We rode along the banks of the Rouge River exploring the trails and surroundings. Some of the paths were good riding and some were demanding because of obstacles like tree roots. I do believe each one of us took the plunge into the river at one time or another, some more than once.

Along our route to Hines we passed an old graveyard, even back then it was old. Sometimes we would stop there, walk around and look at head stones. Even in daylight it was kind of spooky. We found graves from the Civil War, and many from the eighth century. It was maintained, but not much, and occasionally we would see an old man who gave us the creeps tending to things. Just another memory of riding Hines. When we reached Hines we almost always headed northwest, upstream, towards Plymouth and Northville. Once in a while we would go downstream. That direction would lead us to Dead Man's Hill, which we used as a sledding and tobogganing run in the winter. Great fun was had by many families on winter outings there. Only two sides of the hill were used, one side was very steep and stopped at the river. The other was a more gradual even slope and not as bumpy that we used for the toboggan runs. Rumors and lots of variations ran wild about Deadman's Hill and people being killed on the steep side. Our mission when we visited the hill was to walk our bikes up the good side and then ride down. Boy, was that fun! We glided all the way without peddling and just tried to maintain control. The main reason for not riding there more often was the long walk up the hill with our bikes.

The trails along the river were most rewarding for young explores. For us kids Hines Park was our only relief from city life. We enjoyed being along a moving river and with a canopy of trees above, it gave us a feeling we never experienced in city life.

As kids, most of us were always open for ways to earn money. Cutting grass, shoveling snow, picking weeds in neighbors' gardens was the norm. I was one who looked for a better job like a paper route. At age twelve or eleven-and-half (I lied about my age and my folks went along with it.) I began my first route. A Detroit Free Press morning paper. I started at 5:30 a.m., not far from home with twenty eight-customers.

Although it was an older neighborhood with not many fences, that meant the dogs were roaming which turned out to be my nemesis. I started every morning with my papers folded and loaded into my bag attached to my front handlebars and off I rode a half mile to start my route. There were four one way short streets. Dogs were a problem and they were making my life difficult. I decided to arm myself. First I took an old broom handle and cut it down to about three feet, drilled a hole at the end strapped a piece of rope to it to complete my first equalizer. Next I got a squirt gun and filled it with ammonia, wrapping it with rags so if it leaked I would not get wet, completing my arsenal.

Most of the dogs were manageable. However, on the first block there was a German shepherd named Judy that was big and intimidating. Judy only approached me at the house. She would not chase me, a blessing. However, the dogs on the other streets would make chase. My club was effective for them. I only shot my squirt gun a couple times because aiming on the bike was tough. I did connect a few times and it was very effective, making the playing field even.

Collecting on that route was a challenge. I tried to do it on Saturdays with some success but being a morning route I would have to make extra runs hoping to catch my delinquent customers at home. The one problem was Judy's owners. It seemed whenever I tried to collect, no one was home. They were a month behind. I was paying for their paper. That's my money and I wanted it. I rode home feeling defeated and dejected. Entering the house my folks could see my demeanor was not good and asked what was wrong. I began to tell the story about not collecting from one of my customers and about the dog. Dad asked me how much they owed, and I said a whole month. Dad said, "Let's go, get in the car." We drove down Judy's street, and I pointed out the house. He pulled into the driveway. Judy came around from the back of the house. Dad opened his door and reached under his seat and pulled out a ball-peen hammer. Exiting the car he walked directly at Judy. A man appeared from the back of the house. Dad told him to get his dog because if not he'd smash her in the head. Dad gave no ground. I was in awe. He spoke with such conviction. He began telling this man that he owed me money for the paper. The man asked how much and I told him. He was surprised by Dad's actions and did some back peddling. While Dad was holding the hammer in his hand, the man apologized for being behind, paid me and said he will make sure I get paid weekly. Dad also informed the man he should have his dog on a leash. We got back in the car and drove home. I was so proud of my dad! He fixed my problem in a matter of minutes. He was a very stern man, but also a loving, caring man in his own way. That day is a day I never forget. The past due money felt good, too.

Chapter Thirteen

Real Jobs

The things, good Lord, that we pray for, give us the grace to labour for.

—St. Thomas More

I sold my Free Press route, making more money than I paid for it. But I had my fill and lessons learned. My next rung on the ladder of employment was the Livonia Beef House, located on Plymouth Road near Harrison, our street. The owner, Joe, hired me to be one of his kitchen help, for eighty cents per hour. I couldn't wait to get started. Many of my friends rotated through the Beef House. Nobody stayed long in that kind of job. Joe always played the tough guy.

The worst job was pots and pans, where I began. Walking into the kitchen on the first day I was stunned at how many dirty pots and pans were stacked up on the washing table. I was given a quick lesson on cleaning them and off I went. Doing the job right and taking pride in my work was drilled into me by Dad at an early age. Being a quality control engineer at Ford Motor Company his work ethic was embedded into his brain.

I finished off the job in short order. Next was the commercial dishwasher for operation check out. This was a big boxy thing with a door on one end where it was loaded. Large trays were used to load all the dishes, glasses and silverware. They were rinsed with a big water sprayer that removed the leftover food into a huge garage disposal that could grind up almost anything. This was more like assembly line work. Everything needed to be loaded in the correct tray and run through the machine. At completion of the cycle the trays would appear at the other end wet and hot. Finding a spot to put the finished trays was tricky, since I had to keep the machine running. This was a lot of work for a kid that just graduated from elementary school. When my first pay-day came, Joe walked around with small envelopes with our names and deductions on them and our cash inside. I went out back and opened it up. There was a nice little stack of bills. The eighty cents per hour looked better in hand than it sounded. I was happy. Joe considered me one of his better workers. It wasn't long before I was promoted to "fry boy" the next position up the ladder.

One afternoon Joe took me into the back room to the big refrigerator and freezer. He wanted to show me how he prepared the huge pieces of beef they served. The cut was called a steamship round, weighing sixty to seventy pounds. I watched Joe trim the fat off the sides, careful not to cut into the meat, and placed the fat on top of the meat where there was no fat, then heavily seasoned the top. The beef would sit outside the refrigerator for a few days until the fat started turning a little green. At that time it would be placed into an oven and cooked for thirty hours. On completion the beef was removed, the top fat removed and then taken to the special steam table to be sliced for customers. The chef would cut to order around the large bone that ran through the beef. As the meat was cut away the bone was exposed giving it the look of a smoke stack on a ship, hence the name steam ship round.

But the Livonia Beef House served more than beef. My job as fry boy was to prepare and cook the fish and chicken as customers ordered. The batter was made by the cook, I cut the fish and chicken. The chicken was partially cooked before frying, I would then dip it in to the batter and the fryer basket for the proper time. Fish was simpler. It came frozen and all I had to do was defrost and cut the correct amount, and dip into the batter and into the fryer for the proper time, then out to the customer. I also cooked all the French fries for the restaurant. I enjoyed fry boy more than dish-washer and pan scrubber. Some of my friends were losing interest in their jobs and performing poorly with poor attitudes. Joe would not put up with that and some were fired. One of my brightest times at the Beef House was when my girlfriend, Connie Moorhead and friend arrived at the back door and I would go talk with them. They laughed at the way I looked with my apron all soiled, but I thought I was cool.

Finally I was ready to move on. I left the Beef House and went back to another paper route with the *Detroit News*. My new route was big and close to the house. The route consisted of about sixty-eight customers. The route was on Harrison Street south of home, between West Chicago and Joy Road with two other smaller streets, Brentwood and Dover. I could do the whole route in about an hour. It was great and the increase in cash made it even better. Next to my last customer on Harrison was the Dairy Mart ice cream shop owned by two older ladies. This was perfect, because I was moving up to varsity team in Little League football and needed to put on some weight. All summer long I would stop there on my route and get a large cholate malt-that was my weight program. It worked. By the start of football season I brought fifteen more pounds with me.

The ladies at the Dairy Mart were terrific. We became friends. I will always remember them and how clean the store was and that all orders went out perfectly. As a matter of fact, taped to the order window was a copy of the health department inspection report. (I was aware of them from working at the Beef House). Their score was one hundred percent. That score is almost impossible to achieve, but not for these ladies. I was very happy for them because they ran a superb business.

I like to think I too was doing a good job, in the newspaper business. My Schwinn Deluxe was performing great. I picked up the papers around 3:00 p.m. at the station on Plymouth Road, folded them and loaded bags onto my bike. I had saddlebags on the back and a handlebar bag up front.

By folding the papers, I could throw the papers on the customer's porches, except for Sunday and some Wednesdays, that were too big to fold. Tossing papers cut down route time. The trick was to hit the porch. People did not want their paper in the bushes or some-where else. I was lucky that only a couple of my customers requested the paper be put between the front doors. No paperboy tossed the papers in bad weather.

Sundays was a chore. It was the biggest paper of the week and it was the only day the *Detroit News* was delivered by 7:00 a.m. Having an older brother that just started driving was great. I would use what-ever means necessary, like doing some of his chores, cleaning the car, or even cash, to convince him to drive me and usually he would. Then I could do my route in record time even with the biggest paper of the week. My style was to grab as many papers as I could carry and run down only one side of the street with the car following. When I ran out of papers I'd run back to the car and load up until one side of the street was complete then turn around down the other side. On Sunday after our routes were completed, some of us would meet up at a small diner on Plymouth Road, the Clock, and we'd have breakfast. I made good money on my paper route and during the Christmas season, my customers shared their kindness.

Chapter Fourteen

Motor Sports

*Trust your hunches. They're usually based on facts
filed away just below your conscious level.*
                                    —Joyce Brothers

While I was riding my bike through the neighborhood
I noticed hanging from a garage ceiling in the neighborhood something that looked like a go-kart. My
brother Tom went to school with the kid that lived there, Butch
Gram. This machine really caught my attention. I needed to know
more about it, so I went back with Tom to Butch's house.

Butch lowered the car and gave us the low-down on the
machine. It was a quarter midget, not a go-kart. Butch used to race it
but out grew it. I asked him what he was going to do with it. He said,
"Selling it for one hundred dollars." My eyes lit up. I ask Butch if I
could bring my dad back later. That afternoon at Butche's dad looked
things over much better than a young kid could. I jumped into the
seat; the feeling was great. I was hooked! I had to have this machine.
After all the questions were answered and we found out where the
local track and club was located we departed, telling him that we'd
be back with our answer. Dad seemed to be in favor of the deal, but
he wanted to think on it awhile. All I could think about was the car.

I had to have it. My brother and I followed auto racing, sports car, Indy car, stock car and drag racing. We loved it.

Quarter midgets are named that because they are one-quarter scale of a full midget racer. The car looked like a real race car. Dad allowed me to make the purchase. He also said that I would pay half and he would pay half. I was on cloud nine.

After purchasing the car and getting it home our next mission was to join the Livonia Quarter Midget Club. We gathered their information on car rules and requirements. We found out that our car had not raced in a long time and we would have to make updates and modifications.

We listed all needed changes on three-by-five cards and one-by-one they were completed. Dad worked at Ford Motor Company and had lots of connections in many areas. This was a real blessing. We purchased knobby tires from Goodyear that would run at our home track that was dirt. There was only a seat belt in the car so we needed a shoulder harness. The steering had to be changed to a rack-and-pinion type, a big change, but Dad had a connection to get this done, as well as changing the engine from clutch to direct drive. The engine had a muffler, but we knew, for better performance, a tuned exhaust was needed. Dad got that done too.

As the yellow, quarter midget was becoming race ready, something I couldn't wait for, I wondered if the only time I would drive this machine would be at the track. I was wasn't going to get much time behind the wheel. I needed practice and a plan to get it.

My plan was to go to the principal and request permission to drive my quarter midget at the Wilson School parking lot in the summer when it wasn't used much. To my surprise permission was granted, although a hold harmless agreement need to be signed. Then we were good to go. Home and the parking lot were very close.

With my parents' instructions of extreme caution, I began to race in the parking lot. It was so much fun! I could run to my heart's content. I really got to know my car well. I knew on race day with the club I would be racing on dirt, however I was still searching to find the touch, the edge. I always wore my helmet and jacket. I loved my Bell full helmet, white with a black visor, just like the racers of that time.

It did not take long for the kids in the neighborhood to see me running my midget at Wilson School parking lot. Pete Hatkow showed up with his go-kart wanting to run it on the lot. I informed him that I had permission and he would need it too. I was surprised that a couple of days later he shows up with permission. I didn't know at first how to take this addition, but I was accommodating. We did some racing together, though our cars were completely different, but it was competitive. Luckily our engagement did not last long.

As the racing season got closer Dad and I would load up the Midget in the Ford station wagon and run some laps on the dirt at the club. I needed the practice. Dirt was a completely different surface to run on. Going into the turns it was necessary to have the rear wheels sliding outwards but not too far to cause a spin. It took practice for me to be comfortable. I was ready or so I thought. On our first race day at the club I felt good and ready to race.

The racing was divided into heats, with the top finishers advancing to the next heat and finally to the final heat or feature. My first time racing with the club I got a real awakening. All these members had been racing a long time and had spent many hours working their cars. I had a lot to learn and the members were very open to sharing their knowledge. I listened and applied it. It wasn't long before I earned some third place finishes. My skill as a driver improved with every race; nowhere near the top but respectable for first year. I know Dad was having fun watching me race and meeting new people. One of my fondest memories was Grandma Hawk at the track; her lawn chair and sun-bonnet at the fourth turn. I loved to see here there. Grandma always enjoyed our activities. No matter what it was she wanted to be involved.

The club did some traveling. The one contest I always enjoyed was the Rouge Days festival. A track was set up for us right on Jefferson Avenue. Lots of people came to watch us and it was lots of fun, like a festival. On our way back from one of our road trips, a guy yelled to us at a stoplight said that he had a car like mine in his garage. Dad got his number. Surprisingly, about a week later Dad showed up with the new, bright orange Midget the man at the stop-light had told us about. I was in shock! It was a factory built car, not homemade. It was beautiful, and fit like a glove. Dad told me it was something he couldn't pass up. Now we were a two-car team like a lot of other club members.

It didn't take a lot of changes to make the orange Midget ready to race. Now I had a car that looked and ran like all the others. Season two was real fun. The new car ran well, looked good and I added some second and third place finishes along with one first. The new car was smaller and made it easier to load and unload into the station wagon.

The club sold the land in Livonia and purchased an old go-kart track on Eight Mile Road east of Telegraph. This track was a hard surface so we went full time to slicks and a change in driving con-ditions. It was so fare from home and a longer ride to the track. To tell the truth, I missed the challenge of dirt-track racing. My driving career ended after the third season. I was awarded a trophy for the most cumulative points, a nice way to end it all. I grew too big to get into the car, I was growing up. Quarter midget racing was a won-derful phase of my childhood, full of great memories, many with my dad. I always found things to occupy my time, and now my thoughts moved to team sports.

Chapter Fifteen

Football the Little Way

Many fans rush to the stadium to get good seats, then stand to watch the game.

—Anonymous

Little League sports were a big part of my childhood. I participated in baseball, hockey, football and wrestling. Football was my passion. I had two older brothers who I watched play from the side-lines, dreaming of the day I would be on the field.

When that day came I was ready to be a member of the Livonia Hawks freshman football team. We practiced directly across our street in the field between Clements Circle Park and Wilson School, with the skating/hockey rink in the rear. Because our house was so close to the field, my dad let the team keep all our practice equipment in our garage. We also made space in our basement for the doctor to do all physical exams for the team.

It was no wonder with the team name Hawks, and our house a central location, some of the players would ask me if my dad was the owner of the team. I felt uncomfortable when I was asked that question. I just wanted to be another player, not stand out. Our practice went from 4:00 p.m. to about 6:30 p.m. They were tough, but as kids we ate it up. As with any group some had a rougher time than others. We worked together as a group building the team. For the first two weeks I was so sore I took Epsom salt baths and cream rubs in the evening.

At that age I was always hungry. After practice I could have eaten the south end of a north-bound skunk. Mom was always there with a good meal and plenty of it, with lots of cold milk to drink. One of her meals that comes to mind was boiled dinner. Mom cooked potatoes, carrots, onions, and corned beef or beef pot roast with all her seasonings. It made for a wonderful aroma and supper.

Practice continued and our coaches, Norm Kopeikin, Denny Andrews, Buddy Shot (Bruce's dad), and John Lawrence (Jay's dad). They began placing players to positions as best they could with no background experience. I was picked to be a running back/half back. Being a fast runner and small size I could squeeze through small holes in the line. We knew game days were getting closer and the day came to get our full uniforms. We were always excited to get them. They were the best quality; no cheap stuff. The coaches and parents made sure of that.

Practice and the challenge continued, learning our plays and everyone's assignments. For us to be successful we all had to do our jobs. The day finally came on a fall day in 1961. At age nine and seventy-three pounds, I took the field with my teammates. We were about to play our first Little League freshman football game.

I wore number 50 and took the field with the offense. The start of the game was a little rough. However, we came together and things smoothed out. My first run was up the middle for a small gain. I took the hits, trying not to let them bother me. Finally the coach called for an end around play. The quarterback handed the ball to me as planned and off I went. My teammates did their blocking assignments and after I put a few moves on the linebackers, I was gone. Scoring my first touchdown felt wonderful. We went on to win our first game and I scored one more touch down. I learned to keep my legs apart when running and most importantly, hold on to the ball! We ended the season undefeated and I managed to score eight touchdowns, a freshman Little League record. I did not do anything exceptional; I just did what came naturally. I ran and moved, trying to remain on my feet.

The freshman season with the Livonia Hawks was a dream come true for all of us. I could never have had a season like I did if it were not for my teammates. At age nine some big lessons were taught to me that are with me to this day. Work together. There is no I in team. Practice, practice, practice and then practice more. Respect one another. All Hawk teams participated in the Huddle Prayer spoken before the game.

"Grant us the strength, dear Lord to play this game with all our might, and while we're doing it we pray you'll keep us in your sight, that we may never say or do a thing that gives offense to you." I wonder who does the Huddle Prayer today.

In 1962 at age ten I moved up to junior varsity (JV) and the coaches pushed us more. I began to move around experiencing different positions. I played defense as a linebacker and I liked that. It was fun reading the play following the ball, then making the tackle. Playing both defense and offense was strenuous, taking a lot out of me, but I didn't complain. Our first year in JV was good. We learned to lose with pride. Losing is a great lesson as kids. We lost three games that season.

The next year I looked forward to Little League varsity play but I could not make the minimum weight to move up. I stayed a second year on JV. There were a few other teammates that did not make weight either. At age eleven and eighty-seven pounds I started the 1963 Hawks football season at number thirty, ready to go and grow. The coaches wanted to move me to the quarterback position. I was surprised and interested. Quarterback was a new concept for me. Not only did I need to know my position, I needed to know the assignments for all positions. The coaches felt I could do the job. We practiced hard and long, and I was beginning to feel more comfortable at quarterback. However, passing was my big question mark. As our season began, we were working as a team and I was managing my task. My legwork was good and handoffs too, but passing was inconsistent. My biggest challenge was that I was short and had trouble seeing over the linemen's heads. I devised a way of compensating. I knew the routes the receivers were running and I could catch a glimpse of the coverage. I would pick my receiver and let the ball fly.

Surprisingly my system worked and we completed passes, but rarely did I see the catch. But I heard from the crowd. It was fun.

What wasn't fun, was setting up for a pass and getting wacked by the defense. I tried my best to stay away from that. With the crowd yelling, "Go, Hawks!" and the coaches calling, "Hawk," I was getting confused. I told the coaches my dilemma and they came up with a fix. My new name from them would be Shorty, both easy to hear and not confusing. It stuck, and I was not confused. Along with my quarterback duties, I still played defense too. And at the end of the game I felt like I played a complete game.

Every season ended with a banquet for all the Livonia Hawks players, coaches, cheerleaders and families. My dad was given a key to the city of Livonia for his role as a founding board of director for Little League Football of Livonia. Dad never coached, but attended every game, and his contribution got this program off the ground. The night ended with every player and cheerleader receiving a trophy. It wasn't like today, when all kids get rewarded no matter what. We all played as a team and were rewarded as a team, no one's credibility was questioned.

1964 started my first and final year as a varsity player and final year as a Livonia Hawk. At twelve years old I managed to top the scales at one hundred four pounds, mainly due to my stop every day at the Dairy Mart. My number for this year was seventeen, more fitting for a quarterback. Again it was much like previous years, hard work, fun and dedication. My understanding of the game improved, and I was still called Shorty. Four years of Little League football has ended. The lessons and memories aided in molding me into the person I am. My God-given talent and all the social skills experience has blessed me.

The fall of eighth grade there was no football; four years and now nothing. Fall just did not seem the same. I was eyeballing next year and moving into public school football. This year I concentrated on wrestling and ended up as Livonia Public Schools eighth grade one hundred forty-four pound weight class champion. Wrestling is a very individual sport and for my first attempt, I liked it. The matches are short and intense; speed was critical.

Football training at Emerson came early this year. The players were bigger and the game became much more intense. Coaches were tough, having one thing on their mind, winning football games. At one hundred forty-five pounds I had good moves, was steady on my feet and I could take a hit. The problem was the hits were harder, and added up. There was no doubt the game had transformed from Little League. Our scheduled game day was Thursday afternoon, away games we were bussed to the home field school. After weeks of practice and drills we were ready for our first game. Everyone was focused on their assignments and responsibilities. It was an even match up, and our defense was doing a good job of containing. I played a fair game, no touch downs but good running. We went home the victors that day, and we celebrated on the bus ride home. Playing on Thursday afternoon was good for me because Friday was a light practice and I had two days to recover before starting all over.

Coaches from Franklin High School were spotted at a few of our games, so they had a good idea what was coming to them in the fall. For the players starting at Franklin it was the same drill as junior high hell week, only on a larger scale at Franklin. They split into JV and varsity and practiced separately. All JV players dreamed to move up to varsity. This happens but not a lot. At my size I was challenged enough, I just wanted to excel on the JV squad.

The coaches at Franklin positioned me at running back, my most comfortable position. Finally our first real scrimmage was against Edsel Ford High School of Dearborn. We played hard and smart, and won a tough game. During the game I was making an end-around run to the right side and got hit by a linebacker. I felt a strong pain in my left leg during the tackle. I continued playing, though the pain did not let up.

After the game the coach examined my knee and told me to take a whirlpool soak. He explained they would shave my leg and tape it up for every practice and game and I would be fine. Before playing I spent about twenty minutes getting my left knee taped and after, getting untaped, and then spent thirty minutes in the whirlpool. It was necessary but extreme. Having my knee taped was somewhat restrictive and difficult to adjust to. I was able to continue playing doing some good running for the team. However, at this level, size was a major factor. We ended our season in second place, ahead of the varsity squad.

After our final game I was in the training room getting my tape removed, and two of the coaches came in and handed me a piece of paper with a couple of doctors names and phone numbers. They advised me to make an appointment with the one of my choice to have my left knee checked out.

I went home that night and informed my parents. Mom made an appointment for me to see Dr. Young. We were told he was a very good orthopedic surgeon at St. Mary Hospital in Livonia. Mom and Dad both went with me to the appointment. I was taken in for x-rays Dr. Young moved my knee all around and asked me questions, reviewed the x-rays then came to his recommendation. I would need surgery. My knee had cartilage and ligament damage. He recommended not waiting too long. I think we all were stunned and not prepared for that diagnosis. Dr. Young advised us to make our plans then call his office and they would coordinate his scheduling with the hospital. We thanked him and Mom said she would be in touch with his office. On the short ride home we all realized the need to get a plan together.

I was still having a difficult time believing I was going to need surgery. My mind reflected back to the first day my knee was injured. Had I not continued playing would I be in the same situation? A question I still ask myself. We agreed that I would use the Christmas vacation time to cut down on the time away from school. As much as I wasn't happy, it did make sense. I informed all my teachers of the upcoming absence so they could plan any studies for me at home. All my friends were very supportive and would for sure visit me in the hospital and home. That gave me a good feeling. When the day finally came for me to begin my hospital journey we were all ready. Mom had a small bag packed for me, and I said goodbye to my brothers and sister. Mom, Dad, and I loaded into the car and we were off to St. Mary Hospital.

We were directed to the admissions office, then escorted to my room. I was shocked to learn I would be in the pediatric department.

My bed was one of four in the room; the other three beds were occupied. They were more like cribs than a bed. I told my parents this was totally unacceptable and if I could not have a room in the regular hospital I was heading home.

St. Mary Hospital was run by the Felician Sisters based on a teaching, not medical convent. The hospital rules state that any patient under sixteen years of age will stay in pediatrics. I was beyond mad. We loaded back into the car and drove home. At home Mom and Dad talked to me about all the plans that had to be changed. They talked to me in a way only parents can relate to their kids feelings and hurt. After some talking and crying, I changed my mind, and I went back to pediatrics to have my surgery.

Checking in the second time was quicker and I was in my crib in no time. All the kids in my room were much younger than I, in the five to ten years of age range, with not much in common. What hurt me the most in pediatrics was that none of my friends could come and visit me, parents only. That really saddened me. But it was time to focus on my surgery. I was visited by a few doctors throughout the evening and morning hours detailing how all this was to play out. I'm motivated to get this done and move on. Mom and Dad were at my side early that day. When they came to take me to the operating room Mom and Dad gave me a kiss and said they would see me back in my room. I was given an injection before I left my room and I was feeling really relaxed and calm. The last thing I remember was being moved onto the operating table. I woke up after the surgery and was told by the doctor that everything went as planned.

Mom and Dad had a surprise earlier that day. While my parents were sitting in the waiting room for surgery families, they noticed Dr. Young standing nearby. He looked at them with a strange look. Come to find out, that by leaving the day before, my surgery was scratched and was not added back on the list. The change was noted and I was added back on again. Dr. Young accomplished the surgery with no problem. When I returned from surgery the nurses kept the pain away with regular shots. I spent five days in the hospital and after a few days of not shaving I had a good growth of whiskers on my face. I was the only patient in pediatrics in need of a shave. However I refused; my only retaliation for being in pediatrics. I wanted to remind them of my age. I did some physical therapy in the hospital and learned how to walk with crutches, preparing for my return home. I was given some exercises to do at home and a date to revisit Dr. Young. With my crutches at hand and a wheelchair to drive me out of the hospital, I said goodbye.

My siblings were glad to have me back at home. They missed picking on me. Since it was January walking on crutches outside was not a good idea only when necessary. I walked in the house. After a few weeks at home I was ready to go back to school with the understanding to go slow and take it easy. I was easily spotted by my crutches, and heard lots of welcome backs and questions. It was a great feeling having all this pleasantness shown my way. Friends are wonderful. I was working hard on my rehab so I could nix the crunches and resume a somewhat normal life. Over time life became routine and the question of whether I'd continue with my football career at Franklin High School came up. At one of my visits to Dr. Young's office, I asked him if continuing with football could cause me permanent damage. His answer was yes. I was beginning my aviation training and good health was essential.

I chose to end my football career. I was a good player and loved the game. This was not an easy decision. I devoted a lot of my young life to it. Having good health and flying airplanes was my future. I passed on my decision to the coaching staff and players. Most were understanding. What really made me sad was what happened in the early part of the next season. During hell week, some coaches were using me as an example to players, asking, "Are you going to be a quitter like Hawk? You better get tough or you will end up like Hawk." I learned of this talk from some of my closest friends who were still playing. Is this what team sports are all about at the high school level? I think the coaches had a screw loose for using me in a negative way—a player who was committed, dedicated, cared, and always a team player. After everything that took place in my high school athletics, I'm glad I chose to go my way, knowing the true meaning of how the game is played.

Chapter Sixteen

Teen Years

I must take issue with the term "a mere child," for it has been my invariable experience the company of a mere child is infinitely preferable to that of a mere adult.

—Fran Lebowitz

Paper routes turned into real jobs. I learned to master them by getting to work on time, working hard, getting along with others and doing our duties well. This was a new life. My first adult job was at the Livonia A&W drive-in on Plymouth Road not far from home. Pat Thieson, the owner, was a good guy, fair, funny and sincere. Like many bosses when things were busy, his favorite position was ringing the register and at closing he counted the cash. He separated all the silver coins into one bag. At my young age I thought that rather strange. He realized America was no longer making silver coins. I'm sure when the time was right Pat pulled out those bags of silver and made a huge profit.

My first jobs at A&W were to make root beer and to chop a gallon of onions every shift. The root beer was made in a seventy-five gallon refrigerated tank fairly easily. My least favorite job was cutting onions. The onions were delivered to us in fifty pound bags and we needed to precisely chop them into the correct size. It was a challenge. The most fun part of this job was drive-in business and dealing with the car hops. Pairing up young boys and girls at work in a fast-paced job was interesting to say the least. The crew knew that the money was made during rushes and we had to be on our best performance.

Directly across the street from the A&W was a very big GM plant (Fisher Body) where car and truck seats were made and many of the workers were women. Pat had worked hard to develop a good relationship with these people and they filled the place during the four shifts lunch breaks. They had limited time and we worked hard to get their food out quickly and correctly. It was those times we learned how fast time would fly by.

Two other groups that would frequent the restaurant, were Little League baseball teams and city cops. The kids came after a win and the coach or parents treated the kids to root beer. They loved it. The cops were another story. Pat liked to have a police presence at the store and his way of inviting them was to give any on-duty cop free root beer and half-off all food. It was win-win for everybody. Pat Thieson was a good man and ran a good business.

Pat had a couple of friends, Jim and John, who owned the Mama Mia Restaurant just down Plymouth Road from the A&W. It was a very popular restaurant in the neighborhood. The business was started by Jim and John's parents. When they came to A&W it was fun—with good stories, and they treated us well. A&W fit me just right at that time of my life; decent money, good schedule, good boss and crew to work with.

There also was a ski shop directly next to the A&W, owned by Dan Wood. Snow skiing was really starting to take off and Dan's approach catered to the family skiers which most shops did not. After two years Pat bought the Ski Chateau. This was a good fit since both were seasonal businesses and next to each other. Also set up in the shop was a consignment area for customer equipment, boots, skies, poles. The consignment allowed the parents to keep the kids in ski equipment yearly and not break the bank (a great concept). My junior year Pat approached me to work at the Ski Chateau as a ski binding installer. He knew I was good with tools and mechanically inclined. Pat's friend, Steve, said he would teach me and help me if I got swamped or had a problem, I agreed. I went in after school and checked for any skis to be mounted that day, then scheduled times to finish ones for later in the week. I was paid well by the job, so I did not need to be there if there was no work.

My biggest challenge in mounting the skis was that all holes were drilled by hand and depth was critical. Not deep enough and the screws would rip out; too deep and you could drill right through the ski. Touch and feel was the skill. Over time I became a proficient ski binding installer.

Chapter Seventeen

Discovering Girls

Was she so loved because her eyes were so beautiful or were her eyes so beautiful because she was so loved?
—Anzia Yerierska

Girls entered my life at Emerson Junior High School. My first serious encounter was Laurie Wooddack. She was in eighth grade and I was in seventh. I think she had the hots for me. We talked between classes and walked home together. This fling did not last long. She was a fast mover and I was still finding my way with women. Though having a good looking older girl interested in me was a great confidence builder.

I was friends with many girls. One day I spotted a beautiful blonde that I had never seen before. I had to find out who she was and did this by putting word out to my female friends to find out about her. Reports were coming in Connie Moorhead was a seventh grader and had just moved here from Tennessee. It didn't take long and we were having conversations. She still had her southern accent, which I thought was cool as did many others. For me it was love at first sight. Our friendship grew and before long we were passing notes to each other by way of mutual friends. I was getting the feeling that she was interested in me. It wasn't long and I was walking her home after school almost every day. She lived a mile in the opposite direction from school and my house. Those walks with her were worth every step. When we reached her house I would go in and sit with her mom and talk. She was a cool lady. Sometimes her mom would go to the store and we would be alone. Then we would lay on the couch and make out. In my heart I knew this was love I think Connie felt it too. It was the best feeling ever. All our friends told us we were the perfect couple.

On weekends we went to Wonderland Center, the first mall in Livonia. Kids were always hanging out there. One day I took some of my paper route earnings and went to the Cosmetic Shop, a store in the mall that also sold jewelry. I purchased a pearl ring for Connie. I was so happy and could not wait to give it to her. I had it wrapped in a small box, and I surprised her with it a couple days later. She just loved it. I was so happy. A short time later she surprised me with a fantastic ID bracelet with my name inscribed on the front and hers on the back. I still have that bracelet to this day.

Connie's birthday was coming up and I wanted to do something for it. I came up with the idea of a surprise party at my house. I began to organize the details with some of our friends. I also received the blessing from my folks for the bash. I arranged for everyone to pitch in with some cash for food, pop and a gift to insure it would be a fun time. Mom took care of getting and preparing the food. As the day grew closer I was working hard to keep it a surprise to Connie. A large group was coming and they knew how important secrecy was.

I was working on the gift. In talking with her friends I was reminded of Connie's love for cats. A real one was out of the question, so I went with the next best thing, a stuffed animal. I found a four foot, lime green plush cat. It looked great. I picked it up from the store a few days before the party and stowed it in our basement. It was too large to wrap up so I just kind of hid it in a corner.

My folks informed me that my Uncle Don and Aunt Magritte from Superior, Wisconsin would be visiting at our house the weekend of the party. At first I hesitated, but then realized they were both teachers and they know how kids are when having fun. Decorations were in place, thanks to a group of friends. Mom had all the party food ready.

I planned with Connie's mom to have her drop off Connie at seven o'clock. She was coming over just to watch some TV with us, and my dad would bring her home later. All the guests arrived on schedule. The plan was set. Connie and her mom pulled into our driveway in their blue Plymouth Valiant. They entered the house and all the necessary introductions to my family were made.

I told Connie I wanted to show her something down-stairs. In the stairway all was quiet. At the end of the steps the surprise began. All the lights came on with screaming, yelling and laughing. Connie was in shock to say the least. With all our friends around we had a wonderful time. Then came time for the gift. Someone pulled the cat from around the corner and I thought Connie was going to pass out. Just the size of the thing was extraordinary. The party continued with loud music, dancing, singing, laughing and friendship. The adults brought down the food and pop. Things never got out of control. Some of the smokers went into the laundry room and had a few cigarettes, no harm done, nothing said. As with every gathering there is always something that stands out. Connie wore a pair of very tight white pants as was the fad with the girls then. Somehow she ripped the crotch out of her pants. She was so embarrassed. I took her upstairs to Mom and Aunt Marquette's care. Quick repairs were made to the pants and in no time she was back down enjoying her party like nothing happened. The adults were the stars. All good things must come to an end. Dad and I drove Connie and her new cat home. What a good time! Our friends talked about the party for a long time after. I could never have pulled it off by myself. It was good planning, great friends and wonderful understanding parents.

Connie was a very pretty, popular girl. Sadly, going steady ended. Guys were standing in line for a date with her. I guess she had a desire to play the field. We went our separate ways. I know Connie still had feelings for me but her desire to see other guys was important.

It hit me real hard. In my mind, at that time, she was the girl I was going to marry. I remember sitting down in the living room and telling my parents that I wanted to marry her. I was going to build a tree fort and we could live off my paper route. I know it just sounds young, but to me it was very real. It took a long time to recover from that knock, if I ever did. Something else that upset me was my friends, in my defense, saying bad things about Connie, which I ended quickly. I was a popular guy and had many girlfriends and it helped in my recovery from Connie. Although I never had feelings for another girl like I did for Connie. After about six months we did get back together for a while but it just didn't last. We parted again. I must say the second time did help me to deal with the loss.

Time went by and before I knew it high school started at Franklin. My life had lots of fun and occasionally I passed Connie in the halls.

I heard Connie was pregnant, it was true. She was seeing a guy from the class ahead of me. Trying to do the right thing they married, and Laura Anne was born shortly after. Connie was sixteen. She her husband and baby lived with Connie's parents. With their help and understanding, Connie returned to school.

There was a wedding reception/baby birth party at their house on West Chicago. Many people attended and my friends coaxed me to go along. To cope with this situation I got drunk. Later in the evening I ended up in their back yard sitting against a big tree. I was three sheets to the wind. Connie's dad, Tom Moorhead, came outside. I was having trouble holding up the tree. He was concerned about my current condition. My talk with him helped ease my mind. From that point on I had little contact with Connie. I was told that a few years later Connie was divorced.

Chapter Eighteen

The TV War

In the middle of difficulty lies opportunity.
—Albert Einstein

Thoughts of us not having to worry about the Vietnam War were incorrect. We were coming of age while the war was going strong and the draft getting closer. I always loved America and felt grateful to live here. I had no issues with the military.

My love for flying was as strong as ever. I knew that to fly in the Air Force or Navy a college degree was needed, not my cup of tea. The Army was introducing the helicopter tactics in very large numbers and needed men to fly them. Only a high school diploma was needed for flight school. That seemed more for me. However, rotor blades in place of wings would take serious contemplation on my part. In less than a year after graduation I could be a warrant officer in the Army flying helicopters.

As my plans began to filter through family and friends I was met with stiff resistance. I was informed that Army helicopter pilots almost all went to Vietnam and they had one of the highest death rates in the war. Even with all this negative news I still contemplated the move. Looking back now, the one thing that changed my mind was a letter from my cousin Richard, stationed in Chu Lai, Vietnam, a combat support base. I still have that letter to this day. He made it clear that, being a helicopter pilot in the Army is a quick way to die. Flying in the military is not like flying in civilian life. He advised me to keep my flying fun.

That letter and those words stuck with me. The vision of Army helicopter flying seemed less dreamy and more deadly. Yet my desire to serve my country was still strong. So I targeted my interest to the Michigan Air National Guard. I visited the unit at Detroit Metro Airport for a tour and an explanation of the enlistment process. I took a battery of tests both physical and mental. I did commit to the program and took the oath in the spring of 1971. I was scheduled for Air Force basic in San Antonio, Texas, and then to Colorado for fuel specialist school, training to fuel aircraft. My orders would come sometime in May.

I learned early on how the military works. Before I could get to basic training my orders were changed to security police school. I was keeping an open mind. In May 1971 at the Air National Guard base at Metro Airport I recited the oath.

"I, James Hawk, do solemnly swear that I will support and defend the constitution of the United States against all enemies foreign and domestic. That I will bear true faith and allegiance to the same. That I take this obligation freely and without mental reservation or purpose of evasion, and I will obey the orders of the President of the United States and the orders of officers appointed over me according to regulations and the uniform code of military justice, and I will well and faithfully discharge the duties of the office I am about to enter. So help me God." As an eighteen-year-old, my thoughts were mixed. I believed all the words from my heart and soul, though feeling some fear. This was the biggest commitment I had ever made, other than my first Holy Communion accepting the Lord. Only my uncle Lowell in WWII, Cousin Richard in Vietnam, and I were the only ones in my family ever to take that oath.

My orders were sent along with a one-way ticket on Braniff Airlines to San Antonio, Texas. On my departure day I told my brothers and sister I should be home in about six months. Saying my goodbyes to Mom and Dad I made a point to keep upbeat and positive. Still entering the unknown was heavy on my mind. While waiting to board the Boeing 727 I met two guys waiting to leave Detroit for Air Force boot camp. Ricky Perkins and Jim Smith. It was a relief to be in their company. They both seemed like good guys and a friendship began.

Arriving at San Antonio we were directed to an area of the terminal to wait for a military bus to take us to Lackland AFB. People were coming to this area from many different flights and the numbers were growing. What we thought would be a short wait turned out to be a long, long, wait. Finally, we all boarded the bus for the forty-minute drive. By now it was dark and starting to rain. The mood was unnerving, quiet and tense.

Of the millions of people who have joined military basic training no two stories are the same; everyone is different. The purpose of basic training is to eventually bring everyone into one all-inclusive unit. Everyone doing the same thing at the same time and thinking alike. The variance is that it all gets sifted through an individual mind and body, here lies the uniqueness. My story begins that rainy dark night standing on the pad with sixty other guys being verbally harassed and threatened by someone no one even knew. Then ordered to get into a bed and sleep, only to be wakened with more harassment a few hours later. My head was spinning like a top nonstop. All these people with you are unknowns trust vanished. For the first time in my life I truly felt the meaning of being alone and totally on my own. Who was bad, who was good, I didn't know. About the only time we could try to make sense of this life was in our rack (bed) after lights out. In that peace I would pray for strength and guidance, dream of home, wonder if I did the right thing and I cried too. Telling you this is one thing but to truly know, you must be there to feel it. As in life, time heals all and the early lessons in basic fulfilled the story. I do not feel these life lessons could have happened for me without experiencing basic military training. I am grateful in two ways, that during the Vietnam War I was not called to serve there. Nonetheless, I am humbled and grateful that nearly three million Americans did serve and over fifty-eight thousand gave the ultimate sacrifice. We all finished basic training, the bonding force.

Now we were attending regular classes daily with different instructors, not with the DIs, a relief mentally. Some of our classes consisted of customs and courtesies, Air Force history, personnel affairs, military law, and Air Force security systems. Outdoors we did physical conditioning, first aid, drill and ceremonies. As the weeks passed we were given certain privileges in the evenings after chow. We went to "the patio," a place where we bought pop and candy from vending machines, and smoked conversed and relaxed. When we had a good day in the eyes of the DIs, they would give us an hour or so out there and that time was treasured.

The class receiving the most gossip was marksmanship training on the M16 rifle. For most of our class this would be the first and last exposure with a weapon in their Air Force career. However, we all must qualify, to complete basic training. The guys entering security police school knew we would be handling this weapon and many more in the Air Force inventory. After a full day on the range it was back to the barracks.

Back at it again early the next morning into the cattle cars and the drive out to the range. This was the day that counted, all shots would be recorded. Protocol was the same as yesterday. While I was on the firing line my performance was good, above average, my target groupings were tight, firing at one hundred yards ninety percent of the time, though we did some firing from three hundred yards, mainly to show us the weapon is effective at that distance with open sights. At the end of the day everyone qualified—some more relieved than others.

Our time in basic training was getting nearer to the end and we would all be moving to our technical schools soon. I was sitting at the patio reading the San Antonio newspaper and found out my draft number, 115, had been picked. I was relieved and confident I was at the right place.

One other interesting part of my basic training experience was discovering a particular group of trainees we called the fat-boy squadron. These guys were way over the Air Force maximum weight limits. However, the Air Force cut a deal with them and allowed them into the fat-boy squadron to lose the necessary weight. After the weight loss they would be allowed to restart their enlistment at that date. They worked very hard. Everything they did was related to weight loss. I can remember seeing huge trays of celery or carrots sent to their barracks for a snack. This process took months of time and dedication, but most made it through, a win-win for the Air Force.

As our time in basic grew, so did our privileges. One point of interest on base was the Chaparral Club, where we occupied our precious free time on base.

Just before graduation we were allowed a weekend pass to San Antonio, and the boys from Detroit were ready. Jim, Ricky, and I boarded a bus to downtown San Antonio. Getting off near the River Walk we noticed a nice looking hotel the El Presidenta, along the river. We decided this would be a great place to stay.

On pass, we must to stay in uniform, but I never knew the reason for it. Saturday we walked the river. Seeing the gondola-style boats traveling down the river with people relaxing, tranquil and smiling added to our enjoyment. We walked all over town. The cleanliness and the scenes of flowers were abundant. We also stopped at The Alamo, Texas's most sacred ground. We also found a tattoo parlor. This was the only time in my life I came so very close to getting a tattoo. I changed my mind at the last minute. I'm so glad.

After returning to Lackland the next day we all had a better temperament about the place. We were all more tranquil. The last week of basic was much the same, and everyone knew we were leaving soon-everyone except Ricky, Jim and I, and a few others. Our move would be across the street to the home of the security police school. Lackland seemed a letdown after hearing all the cool places the other guys were headed.

A few days before graduation we were allowed to have our stripes sewn on our uniforms. We all made it, no one set back. We moved on to our next Air Force assignment.

goofing off in front of barracks

Sunday goofing off

Chapter Nineteen

Up the Ladder Tech School

*I am only one; but I am one. I cannot do everything,
but still I can do something; I will not refuse to do
the something I can do.*

—Helen Keller

Technical school was set up a lot like a college dormitory
with four men to a room, much improved from the open
bay barracks of basic. Security police were viewed in the Air
Force as a special group due to their mission of protecting Air Force
bases around the world. Our uniforms were maintained at a higher
standard with the fatigues heavily starched, our pants were bloused at
the boot, the only unit authorized in the Air Force for that custom.

Security police is broken into two groups, security police and
law enforcement. I was to go through security police school along
with the other Detroit boys. This training was related to guarding
aircraft, buildings, weapons storage areas, flight lines, missile silos,
and base perimeters. We were told that we were the Army of the Air
Force, the grunts. Yet life was much more enjoyable in tech school.

Other than the time allotted for classes we were on our own and
could even wear civilian clothes after class. To save money we ate dinner and breakfast in the chow hall and bought lunch at the bowling

alley snack bar, cheap and good. The remainder of our cash was for the weekends. Cigarettes, $0.24 a pack; hamburger and fries $1.75; starched fatigues from the laundry, $0.90. My real shock was the pay. After tax deductions, I put $68.64 in my pocket on the fifteenth and last day of the month. Looking back, I wonder how I made it, but I did and had fun too.

During boot camp one of our drill instructors, Sergeant Pollock, our team chief, made an impression on me. He handled himself more professionally than other DIs, firm but not a screamer Sergeant Pollock's Air Force career field was security police. I asked him if maybe we could meet up for lunch sometime, and he agreed. He joined us for lunch at the bowling alley the following week. It was so enjoyable to sit side-by-side with a man of his position and talk. He told us of his duty assignments, and positions he has held. This conversation was so inspiring and uplifting. He had his ego in check and made us feel like men. He was a very special sergeant in my life, willing to take time to help mold a few young men, a true leader.

A week in the field was coming up. This meant the range and firing weapons. The plan was to do as much training for the field in classrooms, like learning to field strip and disassemble the M-60 machine gun, and M-148 grenade launcher. This would allow us the maximum time on the range. I truly enjoyed our time in the field. Firing the M-60 machine gun was my favorite, although I had fun shooting them all. The 60 was able to lay down a tremendous amount of firepower and the person in charge of it was looked after by all troops and they even carried extra ammunition for the gun. When things got bad the 60 was everyone's best friend.

The only malfunction I encountered on the range was with the M-60 on the bi-pod. Sometimes even without a finger on the trigger the gun keeps firing. This is called a runaway gun. The only way to stop it is to let the belt run through the bullets in the gun, or reach over and break the belt feed. My choice was to break the belt and after four or five rounds the gun stopped. This was such an unusual feeling. My brain was saying, "Stop gun," but it continued. For a moment I was scared, and froze, then my training entered into my mind. Everything in the military is based heavily on training and repetition and that is how we learned.

Our time with the M-16 was much more intense than basic. We fired many more rounds and full-auto at different targets. The M148 was the only weapon the Air Force required to be shot right-handed, due to the position of the sight on the grenade launcher. During live fire with the 148, one student did not believe the instructors and fired from the left. The recoil pushed the sight into his nose creating a nice gash. Some people just have a need to find things out all on their own. The M-148 grenade launcher was really fun. It was mounted under the M-16 so it was necessary to elevate the weapon quite high to shoot. Launching a forty-millimeter round, this weapon was awesome. Firing resembles a nine iron golf shot. The shooter can actually watch the round as it leaves the barrel and follow it through the air to the target. To score marksmen with the 148, I had to lay one round from a distance of seventy-five yards away into a fifty-five-gallon drum half sunk into the ground. Having only three rounds and no sights, I had to put one round into the drum. I was able to complete this task and it was a real feeling of accomplishment.

The most carried weapon was the sidearm Smith and Wesson Combat Masterpiece .38-caliber revolver. This was a standard issue for the Air Force in all departments. At first I thought we got short changed because all the other branches carried .45-caliber automatics I learned the .38 was a wise choice. It was a simple revolver with plenty of knock-down power, easy to shoot, safe, and carried by many civilian police departments across the country. We shot many rounds from many different positions until everyone was at ease handling the pistol.

A memorable time on the shooting range occurred during shotgun training for my friend from Detroit, Ricky Perkins. He was really struggling. Ricky had no prior training with guns, like most of us who hunted with friends and family. He was doing well with the weapons training until the shotgun. He was a little guy, only 130 pounds. The shotgun was just overpowering him. He was failing. The instructors saw Ricky's problem, pulled him aside and began to give him special training, working one on one with him. It was quite the sight to see him leaning full forward and firing. Because of special help and care from two of our instructors he passed.

Our final scenario in the field was war games. We split into two groups and all given blank rounds of ammo for our M-16s. The DIs officiated the war. Before starting the battle we were briefed on snakes in the area and told that every poisonous snake in North America could be found in a sixty mile radius of San Antonio.

My excitement for the battle was weakening. In my mind there is no creature I hate more than snakes. They informed us of the rules. When you were "killed," return to the bleachers. If confronted by a snake, instructions were to summon an instructor, by whatever means needed, because they were the only ones with real bullets. I had my plan for this war. I was going to "die" soon. The bleachers sounded much more comfortable than crawling in the grass with snakes. I was the third troop to the bleachers and for me this war was over.

The only causality of the war was my friend Steve Habee, from Lexington Kentucky. Steve was a real gung ho troop and crawled in the grass a lot. After returning from the field he began to itch. His body was covered with chiggers something northerners had never heard of. In pain, he was sent to sick call to find some relief. They were well informed about this problem and he returned to duty the next day. Snakes were not the only enemy in war games.

Our class was invited to visit the Air Force K-9 School. We shared the same mess hall as the dog handlers. At lunch these guys would come in dirty, with uniforms torn and cuts on their arms. Sometimes it looked like they had just finished a street fight.

After spending a day seeing all aspects of training, the dog to the handler, the handler to the dog, I was impressed thinking a dog could be that smart, and I had dogs my whole life. The obedience training was unreal. The dogs only moved by the handlers command and when that command was given there was immediate action. The only time the dogs were trained to move without command was if someone aggressively came at the handler. Lackland was the only base training dogs, and people from all branches trained there. The unit contained anything needed for dogs, including a complete hospital. Their mascot was a wounded German shepherd, veteran of the

Vietnam war. He was credited with saving his wounded handler and also the base under attack by sounding the alarm and was awarded a metal for his actions, spending his remaining years as a hero. The Air Force is so committed to this program they consider a handler and a dog, a two-man team. The reason for our trip was to recruit people to the K-9 corp. It was a big commitment, adding over a year to enlistment time.

Everyone seemed to be performing well as a unit. Time was flying by. It wouldn't be long before our final exams. The true test would be the practical. This test was with real, on-the-job work scenarios as security police officers guarding aircraft, buildings, weapon storage areas, and base perimeters.

Our adversaries would be our instructors ready to challenge our knowledge. I was given the task of guarding an aircraft on alert status, meaning this aircraft was ready to fly a mission, weapons on board. I took up my post and began patrolling, and confirming communications with the command center. The ten series code is used in place of speaking words. This saves time on the radio and helps keep others from knowing what's going on. This system is used by many police forces around the country.

It seemed I had been on patrol forever and not a sound. I even wondered if I may have been forgotten standing out there. Finally, I heard noise from the rear of the aircraft. A man was approaching me at a fast pace. I ordered him to stop. He was talking fast and trying to confuse me. I advised him that he was in a restricted area and being detained. Positioning him on the ground I called the command center, and back-up was sent. At the end of the day we were critiqued. I passed and I was relieved.

The area of training that was drilled into our heads over and over was the phrase "Use the least amount of force necessary for the situation." Those words have stuck with me my whole life. For example, if a guy approaches with a pocketknife, don't pull out a revolver and shoot him. I've even developed a form of this idea in daily life.

Graduation was coming close and the time to receive duty assignments. Those of us in the Air Guard knew we were going back to our home bases for on-the-job training (OJT) to finish our active duty. For the regular Air Force this meant duty assignments anywhere in the world. Four of my classmates drew Vietnam and accepted their assignments well. They would have advanced training before their deployment to Southeast Asia. Most others were assigned to Europe, Asia, and the States.

One assignment I will never forget was to a missile base in Minot, North Dakota. For a classmate who I did not know well. The night assignments were handed out he called his wife and gave her the news of where they would be going. She freaked out and said no way would she go, and she was leaving him. He was so affected by her response he went into the upper bay latrine and tried to take his life by cutting his wrists.

That night I gained great respect for our dorm chief. Before this time I did not think highly of him. Finding out what was happening he ran into the latrine, jumped over the stall wall, opened the door and begin first aid to the airman. An ambulance was called and, he was at the base hospital in minutes. His life was saved. After he healed, he was transferred to "causal," an area where airman waited for assignments or discharge.

Graduation finally came. I was pleased and surprised to finish third in the class of sixty troops. My only response to that ranking was that I listened, applied myself and always did my best. I knew my time at Lackland transformed me. I was in the best physical shape in my life, my mind was sharp, and I grew up and handled responsibility well. In my mind I was a man. I was happy to graduate and hold the position of Security Police Officer.

Chapter Twenty

Homecoming the Military Way

The strength of a nation derives from the integrity of the home.

—Confucius

When I walked off the airliner into the jet way, seeing all the friendly faces huddled together and Mom and Dad off to the side looked great. I was wearing my dress blue uniform and all tanned from the Texas sun. I conversed with my friends for a long time, too long. I was lost in the excitement. Then it hit me, my Mother and Father were standing off to the side waiting to see their youngest son home from the military. Realizing my mistake I went to them. With patience only parents can have, they opened up to me and welcomed me home. To this day my blunder of that day pokes at me. (Honor thy Mother and Father). I did ride home with them and we enjoyed the conversation.

I only had four days before reporting to Selfridge Air Force Base in Mt. Clements. Once again the military changed the plan. While reporting I was informed that all security police personnel were gone. I was then notified that while on active duty at Selfridge, my OJT (on the job training) would be in law enforcement, not security police, not using the training I just completed at Lackland. So goes the way of the military.

I was introduced to the two sergeants that I would be working with. I tried to take this change as a positive. I would be learning something new and could add to my list of experiences. As it turned out I really enjoyed my time in law enforcement at Selfridge. My mentors, both sergeants in the regular Air Force, were very smart, easy going. Part of a few regulars left on base for the transition from Air Force to National Guard control.

There was a small jail at our headquarters, holding mainly deserters from the Michigan area who turned themselves back to the military. The Vietnam War was still on and a lot of draftees were serving. Those were very strange times for our country.

One of my jobs was to mop the floor, not in the cells, but the outside areas. One day I was doing my mopping and from the cell I heard someone call my name. I turned and looked up to see a guy I went to school with and played Little League football with. It was Al Pentergast. He asked me what I was doing. In shock I said, "What you are doing? You're in the cell, not me." We talked for a short time and he told me he had deserted from the Army and was turning himself in. I felt bad for him. However he was well aware of his predicament, and willing to take whatever was to come, and I give him credit in making his decision.

When we had a full jail of prisoners, the Army flew in a Beech 99 aircraft, that I nicknamed "the jailbird,". They were flown to Leavenworth, Prison in Kansas for trial and confinement.

Once a week the Air Force Nightingale DC-9 hospital plane would fly in and drop off the wounded troops. Our job was to stand guard through this operation. A somber time, families would be there to see their loved ones for the first time since they went to war, and it was tough. The most critical were moved first to ambulances, then the walking wounded de-planed.

There were times I felt that I missed something by not going to Vietnam. That duty was the closest I ever came to the reality of Vietnam, and for that I am grateful. God bless the boys that did.

As my training advanced I was given more responsibility. I began to feel like I was contributing as an equal not a trainee. Our road patrols were usually one man on days (except for training), and two men on night patrols. I began to do daytime patrols on my own, and really enjoyed it. Carrying that responsibility boosted my morale.

I learned early on that females were attracted to men in uniform, especially when they were also carrying a pistol on their side. Many of my lunch breaks were at the golf course clubhouse snack bar. Selfridge has a small course on the base, this is quite common at Air Force bases. The food at the snack bar was good, however my main reason to go there was the cute girls. I always thought I was a decent looking guy. The girls there flirted with me like I had the goods. It must have been the gun, but I enjoyed every minute of it.

The best spot for me to pull duty was the main gate. For some reason nobody liked it, but for me it was the best spot to meet girls, even better than the golf course. I was successful arranging dates there almost as needed. One gal I met on gate duty was the daughter of a "full bird" colonel. We hit it off right from the start. I saw her coming through on a regular basis. She would pull into the side parking and come up to talk more. We made plans to meet after I was off duty, a relationship was beginning.

One evening after I was done working I decided to take her to my home area, which was Livonia. I wanted to show off the spots I frequented. The only problem, Livonia was an hour-and-a-half drive from Selfridge, and the time was early evening. We made the trip. I showed her the hot spots and met some of my friends.

Then the realization came to me that she needed to get back to her home on base. I didn't want her dad, the colonel, hunting me down. I convinced my buddy Galen Wolfe to drive with me to help keep me from falling asleep. Galen reminds me of that trip to this day. He was not happy that morning, but what a great friend.

The only time I ever pulled out my pistol was one evening on patrol. We received a call that the base finance building alarm was going off. We rushed there with no lights or siren. Arriving, we found the interior lights on. The sergeant directed me to go around to the back and he would go in the front. From the back I did see movement in the building. The pucker factor skyrocketed; it seemed like the real deal.

I was so relieved to hear from the sergeant that it was a false alarm. The movement I saw in the building was the cleaning man. This run upset me. How did it get so screwed up that someone could have been shot or even killed? I was more shook-up after than during the whole event.

Another memory comes to mind. One afternoon we received a call of a domestic disturbance at the base housing. Arriving there we found a couple on their front porch in a heated battle. (These are the calls no one likes to get.) She wanted him out and now. We observed signs on her of a physical altercation and he had been drinking. Due to this, he was detained and taken to the station. Now with him out of the picture she began to throw all his clothes out on the porch, saying she is going to burn them up. I explained to her if she does that she will be arrested for a much more serious offense than her husband, and finally she came to her senses.

We also had responsibility for an off-base government-owned housing subdivision about ten minutes from the base. We made regular patrols there, and things were for the most part quiet. These trips helped break up the daily routine. As my active duty time was coming to an end, I was okay with that. Going home and attending weekend drills once a month sounded good.

I enrolled at Schoolcraft Community College, feeling that was the thing to do. My heart and head were not in it. My grades and attendance showed it. I spent more time playing euchre in the student union than going to class. I only lasted two semesters.

When I first returned from Lackland two friends from the old neighborhood, John Watterson and Mike Marocco, stopped by. They wanted to know all about the National Guard since both pulled very low numbers in the draft lottery. I told them my story and feelings about the Guard. A few weeks later I heard that they both joined the Army Guard.

My time in my Guard unit was draining my upbeat positive attitude. Weekend after weekend the same old thing, standing inspection every morning to active military standards and then hanging around looking like you were doing something with no real mission. The only worthwhile assignment I was called to perform happened to be security around an aircraft incident on the base. Our unit was transitioning into F-101 Voodoo aircraft. One of our pilots, returning from a training mission mistakenly deployed his drag chute around one hundred feet above the runway while landing. He crashed alongside the approach end of the south runway. My job that night was to keep everything, including animals from the crash scene. Nothing was to be moved until crash investigators arrived in the morning. It was a long cold night, securing the remains at the scene.

The weekend drills marched on and I enjoyed it less and less. The hardest thing for me was the inspections. My hair-cut had to meet strict military standards. I was pulled from ranks and sent to the barber shop more than once. This was the early seventies and longer hair was fashionable, military service was two days a month but having to meet their dress code for the whole month was very upsetting. I did not want hair down my back, I just wanted to have a little hair over my ears.

Through the grapevine word was out that the 305 Air Force Reserve unit at Selfridge was looking for loadmasters on their C-130 aircraft. This position was a NCO (noncommissioned officer) crewmember. The responsibility of the loadmaster is basically in charge from the cockpit back of all loading, unloading, aerial dropping, and any duties related to the cabin, directed by the aircraft commander. Flying on weekend drills would be perfect. I made contact with the unit and setup for an interview. Walking onto their base operations and seeing the C-130s on the flight line gave me goose bumps. I was met by the sergeant in charge of the loadmaster section and escorted to their operations area for an interview. I informed him I was a private pilot and had been around airplanes most of my life. He ended the interview by inviting me on an introduction flight, their schedule had an opening in two days; in the late afternoon. I responded that I will be there. My outlook for the military was looking up.

I arrived early the day of my flight. I wanted to show my extreme desire to be a part of them. I was introduced to the loadmaster I would be flying with and shadowing on the trip. He was a bit older, but very talkative and open. I was shown the loadmaster's equipment, both personal and aircraft. Heading to our aircraft I met the rest of our crew, A/C commander, second in command (co-pilot), flight engineer, navigator and the other loadmasters.

After ground checks and run-up we were airborne, heading out over Lake Erie towards Buffalo, New York. The cockpit crew were doing their thing up front and in back we were doing ours. We all wore headsets for continuous communications. They demonstrated all necessary checks to be made in-flight by the loadmaster. No cargo was on board, which made for a lot of room in the back. We climbed a ladder after moving up front to observe the cockpit. The view was impressive to say the least.

Driving home after the flight I reviewed all my options. One big consideration in transferring to the Air Force Reserves versus the Air Guard was the fact that in the Air Guard I could only be called to active duty as part of my complete unit, meaning our whole unit would receive active duty orders to be deployed. In the Reserves, I could be called up by job classification, meaning if the Air Force needed cooks, or pilots or loadmasters I would receive individual orders for active duty; a serious consideration.

The day arrived for our next meeting to seal the deal with the 305th. I decided to take my chances with the active duty difference. Flying was the goal and feeling like I was contributing to something of value. The meeting opened with them stating that my review by their office was fine and everyone liked my attitude and abilities.

Now the bomb-shell hit. There was one additional requirement to make the transfer complete. I would have to do an additional weekend of duty per month, basically doubling my enlistment. I informed them that I would more than likely end up doing the extra time, however I did not want to sign and make that an obligation. This was a requirement. The deal fell through. I was heartbroken. Something so close that I loved so much was not to be. I was shocked that they waited so long to lay the big one on me, but that's life in the military.

So it was back to security police and not a thing changed. There was talk of our unit getting F-106 fighters with nuclear capability. That thought concerned me.

At a party I ran into my friends John and Mike who joined the Michigan Army Guard. Their story of military life was completely different than mine. Their hair was longer than the normal military haircut. Their stories of their drill weekends were also a lot different than mine. After telling them my situation, they suggested I transfer to their Army unit.

At first I wrote off their idea. No one moves from the Air Force to the Army. As time went on, remaining at E-2 rank, no promotions insight and enduring relentless inspections, as well as boredom, the Army was looking brighter. Pulling duty with my friends, wearing my hair longer, and working in a more relaxed atmosphere, was making more sense.

My friends did some work on their end and secured for me a transfer request to their unit, the 156 Signal battalion in Monroe, Michigan. During my next drill weekend at Selfridge I took the letter of transfer to my CO. He directed me to another office to sign papers. That was my last day in the Air Guard. I was amazed how quick it happened.

The next month the three of us drove to the armory in Monroe for my first drill weekend in the Army Guard. Entering the building there were the troops standing around sloppily dressed, waiting for an order to assemble. Finally, a group of officers and senior NCOs entered the building, ordering us to form ranks for inspection. This formation was like no other with troops with hair down to their collars, uniforms messy, and people standing carelessly at attention. The commanding officer and his group walked through the ranks as if everything was quite normal and acceptable. My Air Force security police background reinforced the seriousness of inspections. This scene, so bogus was just the beginning of my impressions.

Signing into the unit (156th Signal battalion Michigan Army National Guard) locked me back into the Guard. Being released from the Air Guard had put me at risk of being ordered to active duty, if not picked up by another unit. I was issued all the Army gear and told that my new position would be a lineman, climbing poles and running wire, a position I never trained for or ever performed.

Acclimating to the Army was so easy. Relaxed was the word and I was getting comfortable with the events and leaving the rigors of the Air Force behind. Our commanding officer was Lieutenant MacGlocklin, a fairly young man with different ideas. Sometimes it appeared he ran the unit like a Little League football team. Month after month things did not change and the looseness of the unit continued. My friends, John and Mike helped me transition to the military unit ruled by none. One weekend we were scheduled to convoy to Battle Creek, Michigan for training, leaving on a Friday night. Drivers were assigned to trucks, and I was an assistant driver riding shotgun, making sure all necessary equipment was on board. With the coolers filled, and sports equipment packed and a bag of civilian clothes, we were off.

Convoys with this group were loose, meaning spread out all over the road. As we pulled into our scheduled rest stop area, Mike pulled out a beer and took a big gulp. It wasn't long before I saw Mac, our CO heading our way. Stopping in front of Mike he grabbed the beer and tossed it like a throw from center field to home plate. He then laid into Mike like I have never seen before. I didn't think Mac had it in him; even Mike was stunned. We entered our trucks with little being said and continued our journey down I-94 to Battle Creek and Fort Custer. This base was used during WW II for basic training and also as a POW camp holding German prisoners. On our arrival at Fort Custer, Mac approached Mike and said in a calm voice that he should not have been drinking in a public place, then handed Mike a fresh beer. This was Mac.

Summer camp with the Army Guard was held at Camp Grayling in north central Michigan, a very beautiful area. John and Mike had been there before and told me they knew the routine, so I followed. Not being assigned a truck to drive we all piled into Mike's new Thunderbird and headed north.

Our first stop in Grayling was at the Holiday Inn and into our civilian clothes. We went to the bar to wait for our company and trucks to arrive on post. This was a very different start for summer camp for me. I was cautious and curious but enjoying the good life, too.

Later that day we went to our company assembly area in the field. We just walked up and blended with the troops. Everyone was busy setting up equipment. After making sure we had proof of making contact with enough people to show our presence, we were back at the Holiday Inn. Thinking how unbelievable this story was just added to the excitement and fun.

Some days we just stayed poolside and never showed up at all in the field. However when we did, we just eased into the company area and made like we were always there. If anyone questioned us, we would play stupid and act like the person didn't know what they were talking about. Our system worked. We also found that we were not the only troops playing this game for the two weeks of camp. We even drove home on the middle weekend. We were informed on the day before the end of camp that our unit was visited by an inspection team at night and there were only five troops manning the company field area.

The worst part of the whole time for me came when it was time to pack up and return to Monroe. Someone had to drive a truck home. John and Mike picked me and I wasn't happy with their choice. So off they went in the Thunderbird. I went to pick up my ride, a two-and-a-half ton truck called a duce-and-a half. I was also pulling a trailer; bad news for speed, but I took my medicine.

All the trucks were lined up for the trip home. We were being lead on a wild goose chase by someone in the lead passing exits from the base to I-75, and just driving around, like on a sunny Sunday afternoon. I was done with this game. I took the next road out of the base. I noticed two trucks still following me. At first I felt bad. They could have turned back. Further down the road I pulled into a rest stop and met my followers. We decided to just make our way back to Monroe. Mike and John held to their promise and were waiting to take me back home to my real civilian life.

At our next drill weekend there was a lot of chatter about our performance, or lack of performance at summer camp and just how things in general were going in the company. The talk became reality. The next month Mac was gone and we had a new CO to save the company from all the evil within. His name was Lieutenant Paul Wilson and he was ready to make a name for himself by making Company A 156th Signal Battalion his shining star.

Everything changed within an instant. Inspections were as hard as or even harder than the Air Guard, adding training, testing, and OJT. No more idle time and trips to the local bars. John and Mike's reputation was very well recognized. I was considered their tag along. Due to this reputation we were Lieutenant Wilson's first targets, and he was well briefed.

The loose inspections were gone, normal military rules were in place. Our dress was not that far out of line from all the other troops, but the Lieutenant went directly to us and removed us from formation. His options were to send us home or to the barber shop for a haircut. This treatment was used on us routinely to be an example to the rest of the troops. Five units (one day was two units) unexcused within one year meant order to active duty. We reached this limit quickly.

I received a letter from the Department of Military Affairs, Director Army, dated September 2, 1975, informing me they found cause to have me return to active duty. We received orders to active duty for twenty-four months at pay grade of E-2 and more than likely going to Germany. I was in shock. My life was in a tailspin. I could not comprehend what life in Germany as an E-2 would be like or if things could get any worse. Mike informed John and me that he went to a doctor who sent a letter to the Department of Military Affairs. His discharge was being processed. John and I followed suit.

The only doctor that came to my mind was Dr. Reive, the doctor who brought me into this world. I explained to him the complete story. He responded to the military in a letter explaining that if my current state of mind persisted I would probably desert or get into serious trouble. His recommendation was to transfer me to another unit to complete my obligation or be discharged. On April 6, 1977, I received a general discharge under honorable conditions from the Army National Guard. My total time of enlistment in the Air National Guard and Army National Guard was a total service of five years, eleven months, twenty-six days.

I am not ashamed of my time served. I enlisted as a teenager. I willingly served, and the tarnish from the Army Guard still tugs hard on me. I was a good soldier with good intentions. We were all caught up in strange times as a country and as a people.

Chapter Twenty-One

Income Flying

Eternal Lord, who makest the winds and clouds obey Thy will and protectest them eagle in his flight and the dove seeking safety, uphold me as I soar into the sky and fly above land and sea. Pilot my ship safely through the air and give me nerves which are steady and relaxed, a mind, calm and composed, as I sail on to my destination. Give me a successful takeoff and at journey's end a safe landing, that no harm come to me and those entrusted to my care.

Hold thy protective hand over me as I pass through storm and clouds and let me not lose my way as I fly by instrument through fog and darkness.

Above all, keep me in Thy grace and favor for Jesus' sake, and let my last landing bring me safely into Thy presence, redeemed and saved to praise Thee eternally and forever. Amen.

—Prayer for the Aviator, Lutheran prayer book, 1951

My time flying for compensation started at Timoszyk Aviation, performing scenic rides and some charters, mainly in single engine Cessnas. However, in my mind it started with Bentley Flight Service on the north ramp at Metropolitan Airport.

While reading the *Detroit News* classified ads, something caught my eye: "Co-pilots wanted, 135 Charter operation based at Metro Airport." The ad read like a dream come true. I quickly phoned and set up an interview with the chief pilot, feeling this was my chance that I had dreamed about for years. I reviewed in my mind everything that could be asked about my attitude, abilities and convictions. I would be ready.

Arriving at the airport early I found the office of Bentley Flight Services. During my wait a man came from an office across the room and walked right into a pole. In my nervousness I made a sound after hearing the thud as he hit the pole. He shouted my way, "Do you think it's funny when a blind man runs into a pole?" "No," I responded, devastated and embarrassed. He passed by me and entered an office off to the side. Jeff Kilponen, the man behind the desk, said he was the owner, and he should have been using his cane. At that point I felt doomed, with no chance for employment. Soon Jim Irvine, chief pilot, introduced himself as we entered his office. He began asking me questions in a very relaxed way, about my flying experience and my life in general. He also reassured me about the situation with the blind man.

He explained why they needed co-pilots. Their equipment was all certificated for single pilot operations. However, their business involved General Motors assembly plants in Canada. The Canadian regulations required a three axis autopilot or a copilot to fly in (IFR) instrument conditions in Canada. The company decided it would be too costly to install autopilots in their old Beech 18s, so co-pilots were their answer. The chief pilot invited me on a flying trip later that evening as a passenger to get a good overview as to what the job entailed. I answered him without hesitation, absolutely. We departed at midnight in a 1950 Beech 18, N24K the pride of the fleet.

The sight of the Beech sitting on the dimly lit ramp with its nose sticking upward, and its big round motors hanging from each wing and its twin tail so close to the ground with the tiny tail wheel gave me an inkling of how different this new experience would be, and could be very intimidating. Captain Dave Brunsguarrd arrived and he started to file our flight plan, and set up the loading. Many of these loads took up most of the available cabin space. I learned that until the freight is on the ramp we never knew what we'd carry.

With all preflight work completed we boarded the plane. In order to read the check list we used small overhead lamps that adjusted to clear or red illumination. As the starter engaged the prop turned through six or seven blades, creating a roar and flames from the exhaust as the radial engine came to life. After repeating the same sequence on the left side, we were ready to taxi and pick up our clearance to Oshawa, Ontario, receiving taxi instructions from the tower.

Not only was the cockpit foreign to me but also Metro Airport, on the ground at night. Satisfied to only be a passenger on this flight, I already felt behind the power curve. We departed runway 21C and climbed into the eastern darkness.

Captain Dave, or Brunsy, controlled all the flying and radio work. I was enjoying good conversation while reviewing the cockpit. My mind was even more bewildered as the flight progressed. This flying is so different from my flight training. No regimented, repetitious lessons tonight. This was wide open discovering time. I questioned myself, had I really gone to flight school?

The approach to Oshawa and landing completed as scheduled, we then cleared customs. A truck from the GM plant unloaded us. This freight is usually "hot," meaning the plant or line could shut down without this shipment, a major sin for the car factories. On our way back to Metro, Brunsy let me take the controls for a while. I flew for about a half hour; did okay, acceptable. Brunsy seemed pleased with my first time performance flying the Growler (another nickname given the Beech 18).

Jim Irvine called the following afternoon. He would like to have me on board and get me on the schedule. On this day January 20,

1977, my dream and my goal was reached as a paid crewmember with a small airline. It felt so good.

The chief pilot shared his summary of how my position would develop, first as a flying trainee and ground school. Then I would take my check ride with the FAA when he and other captains felt I was ready. This would be a second in command evaluation in the Beech at Willow Run Airport. It all sounded good to me. My pay started at twelve dollars per flight hour including a small per diem paid when away from base. I knew that this compensation would be tough, but the true reward is that the knowledge, experience, exposure and joy will be endless. Being one of the first co-pilots hired, the rotation of the schedule changed quickly. Every flight became a new encounter, filled with experiences and education.

Learning to control a ten-thousand-pound twin-engine tail dragger on the ground, with only ten hours total tail dragger time logged, told the story. My first taxing seemed an impossible task, using differential power and brakes along with the rudder pedals, as the only means of control. To master this requires knowing when to use the correct input at the correct time, the wind made this battle a real challenge. The object of this task is to keep the aircraft traveling down the center of the taxiway. My attempts were more like doing s-turns, adding power on one engine then reducing on the other, all the time increasing speed, then braking. In the beginning I felt more like a gymnast, bathing in my own sweat, seeking to master this skill. Fortunately, the captain would take back control just before I would completely lose it, putting things back in proper control. My taxiing improved with time. However, the golden rule prevailed, "Never stop flying the Beech until the parking brake is set."

The beginning days flying the Beech were somewhat standard. In the air the tailwheel means nothing. The controls respond well and she trims out fine. She is a very stable flying machine but the layout of the cockpit panel confused me. These were not modern aircraft. Most of our fleet were fifties, to early sixties era airplanes. Instruments were removed and others added, and made for a confusing mix of layouts. I was discovering the lessons of real world flying and loving it. Another measure of my previous flying included minimal night flying. Most of these flights were at night. Night flying is very different, almost like instrument flying. Night flying gave me the feeling of desolation and exploration, a oneness like being suspended in space. This newness kept me in awe.

The company "milk run" was to Oshawa, Ontario, east of Toronto. Our cargo consisted of auto parts. Sometimes we carried a single box on board, or a load so big it could barely fit into the Beech. It seemed like everything we dealt with was hot. It wasn't long before I had our routing/flight plan committed to memory. I could read back our clearance from ATC without hesitation.

the Queen

Chapter Twenty-Two

The Official Line Pilot Check Ride

We learn according to what you bring into the situation.

—Anonymous

With some prepping by the chief pilot and continually repeating takeoffs and landings, I was recommended for my official FAA check ride. On June 14, 1997, I demonstrated satisfactory ability to pilot a Beech 18 N24K (tailwheel) before Aviation Operations Inspector R. C. McGarry, at the Flight Standards District Office 63, Willow Run Airport. It was official. I received my letter of competency from the FAA. Boy did that feel good! The ride with Mr. McGarry on board went surprisingly smooth. He even complimented me. My trips from then on held a greater significance, as a contributing licensed crewmember. I did not acquire a wealth of knowledge. I was now given legal rights to learn to fly the Beech. A learning process that will be never ending.

As challenging as taxiing was, landings were equally difficult. With tailwheel aircraft there are two techniques in landing. The three point landing touches down on all three wheels at the same time, with low airspeed; a technique utilized in lighter single engine taildraggers. The other is a wheel landing, approaching with more speed and touching first on the main wheels, then reducing speed and slowly lowering the tail down. I knew very few pilots who three point land a Beech correctly. Wheel landings were the preferred technique. Touching down smoothly on the mains while carrying some speed isn't easy. The curve ball comes when touching down too hard. The mains bounce the plane back into the air, pulling off some power. It sends the plane down and the sequence starts all over again. I coined this the "bouncy bounce." The Beech will keep any pilot humble.

I'm having a love affair with the Beech, which brings to mind a particular flight. This took place in August on a lengthy trip, starting in daylight and ending in darkness. The beauty of this trip came over Lake Ontario. By now it was the middle of the night with a moonless pitch black night. Suddenly I spotted a flash through the windscreen, and then another, and another. I realized we were in the middle of a meteor shower. We were observing one every five to ten seconds; long ones, short ones, bright ones, dim ones, colored ones, from all over the sky. Mother Nature was at her best. We were in the perfect position to watch.

On another trip with my favorite captain, Sufu Nana in Beech 675D, it was a nasty winter day, with low visibility, big winds, ice and snow. We executed the VOR instrument approach into St. Clair County Airport, breaking out of the overcast and having good visibility. The only runway open happened to be the north/ south and we had a strong crosswind from the west. Completing the landing checklist and setting up on final into the north, with differential power and rudder control, things looked okay. On touch down we realized how icy the runway was. As the power came off, the noise began to weather vane into the wind, the braking action was poor. We began to slide down the runway cocked into the wind, with large snow banks on both sides of the runway. Our redemption came as the airplane managed to stay on the runway until we came to a stop. Someone had control of that airplane and it wasn't us. We were able to continue the trip uneventfully.

Our normal trips were out and back. On occasion the customer requested multiple trips. This was the case with Harrison Radiator. They had problems and needed help. This time they called to see if we could make multiple flights to Dayton Ohio. Harrison Radiator would be shipping cases of a/c condensers from Detroit to Dayton. We started flying two Beeches a day, two trips each, to Dayton. On one of my trips down a thought came to me. My Aunt Carole and Uncle Lowell lived in Dayton and it would be wonderful to see them. I made arrangements with them and got the okay from the company. My Uncle Lowell picked me up at the airport and we continued to their home. As usual Aunt Carole prepared a wonderful meal. We spent the rest of the evening talking about family and having some laughs. Uncle Lowell dropped me at the airport in the morning. This was one of the last times we were together.

Few trips were done on the weekends, however on a Saturday I received a call from Doug, the dispatcher, informing me of a trip to New Orleans delivering marine paint. This will be a money-maker for us, good training for me and fun, too.

By the time I arrived at the office Doug had confirmed the trip. The Beech we would be flying was 675D, the newest aircraft to the Bentley fleet. Jim Burns, the owner, qualified for and received a Small Business Administration loan to buy it. He installed a new complete radio package, a King Gold Crown set with digital read out and all the latest bells and whistles.

While the tanks were being topped off, I cleaned the wind-screen. This was something I always did with all prefights, I liked clean windows, instead of staring at smashed bugs and whatever else was stuck there. The captains liked to rib me and have fun with my clean window fetish, however no one ever complained about the view.

Our buckets of paint showed up and we loaded them onto the cabin floor. Off we went to New Orleans, Louisiana, Lake Front Airport stopping in Memphis to refuel. Cruising at seven thousand feet in smooth air. I noticed the VOR stations were very weak and almost unreadable. I informed Safu, and he responded, "Lock in your heading after passing the station and hold it."

One of Safu's numerous and outstanding characteristics is that he never gets worked up. He never loses his cool, and always keeps it together no matter what the scenario. As a young first officer there is no other captain who in this learning position ever made me feel more a part of the cockpit. He valued my presence. It was a privilege to fly beside him as part of my aviation journey.

Approaching Lake Front Airport the radios were still weak. The controller asked if we would accept a (GCA ground controlled approach). We accepted. The weather was hot, humid and foggy. While Safu was flying I enjoyed watching the approach coming together (my first GCA approach). After landing we taxied to the offloading area and called for the fuel truck. A delivery truck pulled up to unload us and four guys walked up to the plane. The paint was unloaded in no time. This group invited us to stay on their boat. These guys had a strange look and were not giving off a warm fuzzy feeling. Thanking them for the invite to their boat we explained we needed to push on to Memphis. All I could envision was waking up on their boat and seeing nothing but water all around us. A relief overcame me as we climbed out and left New Orleans. Landing in Memphis in the early morning, we checked into a hotel and after some needed rest enjoyed a good meal.

The final leg of the trip went fine. A lot of flying in two days. The maintenance people informed us our radio problem came from a loose antenna connection.

happy guy

Chapter Twenty-Three

They Will Fly on One

*The real value of twin-engine aircraft is it will dou-
ble your chances of engine failure.*
— Anonymous

Our trip to Memphis was memorable but our trip to Kansas
City was a truly "come to Jesus" moment. It took place
on an unusually warm, foggy, still fall night. The freight
was hot. To our amazement the truck with the cargo was full of auto
header panels (the sheet metal part that fills in the spot between the
hood and grille). This is a large part and there were a lot of them.
We informed our dispatcher that to take all of this load they would
a need at least a DC-3. So they asked us to take all we could get on
board and go. We stacked as many as possible into the cabin, leaving
just enough room at the top for us to crawl into the cockpit.

Some Beaches have emergency hatches for quick exit from the
cockpit, ours had none. This trip to Kansas City started out oddly and
the weather added to the strangeness. Climbing over the cargo to reach
the cockpit, we begin the start check-list. At the time Metro was reporting weather above landing minimums, but visibility was extremely poor.
Cleared for takeoff we began our roll, lifting off uneventfully. Detroit
departure control confirmed we were in radar contact, and flying on

the gauges. I sensed the airplane yawing to the right, and the right tachometer was winding down. The right engine began shutting down. Brunsy called for the emergency checklist and I relayed it to him. By the time we got to "feather prop," the prop is going into feather on its own. We were flying straight and level and holding altitude. This was my "come to Jesus" moment. I prayed, Lord please help us through this danger, keep us safe and I promise to be a better person.

Declaring an emergency and informing ATC of our dilemma, we needed to get on the ground, requesting radar vectors back to Metro but Metro is below landing minimums. We looked at each other in disbelief. We just departed there less than fifteen minutes ago. Next, our plea went out for the closest airport above minimums. Our options were slim. The only viable one was Willow Run with weather that measured four hundred foot ceiling and three-quarter mile visibility; above minimums but not by much. We paused for a second and agreed to take it. ATC responded with a new heading for us to the ILS 23L approach into YIP (Willow Run). The pucker factor was pegged. (Pucker factor is a slang phrase used to describe the level of stress and/or adrenaline response in a dangerous or crisis situation. The term refers to the tightening of the buttocks caused by extreme fear.) Brunsy was doing a great job controlling the Beech. This approach must be flawless. As the controller vectored us to the runway, the localizer came alive (the left and right guidance to the runway). He cleared us for the approach.

At the outer marker, a distance about five miles from the end of the runway, he instructed us to contact Willow Run tower. Clearing us to land, and informing us the fire trucks were standing by. Now Brunsy intercepted the glide slope (giving the pilot the up-and-down direction to the runway). He had us in the slot, with landing check list complete and gear down, but no runway in sight. This was going to be close and a go-around almost out of the question. With Brunsy's eyes glued to the panel monitoring the instruments and me looking for the ground, the lead-in-lights on runway 23L came into view, and shortly after, the runway lights. I called out, "Runway in sight."

Brunsy shifted his view from the panel to the windscreen and confirmed runway in sight. As we passed the threshold and touched down on terra firma the fire trucks followed us, until we came to a stop on the runway. The release of tension was huge. Exiting over our cargo was just as difficult as getting in. We managed to acquire some small cuts from the sharp edges on the panels as we got to the ground. The firemen were doing their thing. We walked over to the starboard engine and observed a large amount of oil covering the cowling. We needed to get this crippled airplane off the active runway. The only thing in our favor, the winds were nonexistent. Brunsy decided to taxi her off the runway to the ramp with one engine running. He felt that he would have no problem with this maneuver, and he didn't. Now our efforts were changed to getting the freight off the airplane.

We skirted legalities with this load. Adding to the fact that we were in the backyard of the FAA, it was imperative we empty this airplane before they came looking for the Beech that had flown in on an emergency. Brunsy called dispatch to get a truck out now to offload us. Surprisingly, the truck arrived at the airplane in less than an hour and the transfer made. Ironically, a new crew flying a Lear Jet picked up the load. The crew loaded less than a third of our cargo, climbed in, buttoned her up and blasted off to Kanas City.

I felt our efforts that night were treated so casually, even though the mission was not completed, our efforts were enormous.

The final report concluded that a valve hung up in the number four cylinder in the starboard engine. The rotation of the engine pressurized the case, pumping the oil overboard, through the vent tube. This caused the prop to start into auto feather. But that night will always be with me, knowing my guardian angel was by my side watching over me. In less than a week the Beech was back on the line and so were we.

Chapter Twenty-Four

How Do You Say "Ice" in French?

I'd rather be lucky than good.
—Dave English, *Slipping the Surly Bonds*

A nother memorable trip was my first trip to Montreal, Canada in Beech N24K with Gary Poge as captain. Gary, a good guy, just a few years my senior, came to Bentley with more total time and multi-engine time than me. His rise to captain occurred quicker. As a new captain his limitations were higher than a more experienced captain and rightly so. With the new captains utilizing higher limits this also raises the FO's limits. If it were my leg to fly and the approach seemed too difficult for me, he would do the approach.

Our trip to Montreal took place in November, an appropriate time in the north for changing weather. Our landing at Montreal (Dorvall) Airport completed, we taxied to Customs. Hearing French on the radio was odd to me. Flight school taught me that English is the universal language in aviation; I guess not so with the French Canadians. We unloaded our freight destined to the GM assembly plant in town.

We strapped back into 24K, picked up our clearance to Detroit and were off. On climb out we entered an overcast area. Gary was flying and noticed we were picking up some rime ice on the leading edge of the wings. It was still daylight and we had a good view of the wings.

The Beech is equipped with the necessary equipment for icing conditions with electrically heated props, carburetor heat, alternate air source and pneumatic boots on wings and tail surfaces. The accumulation of rime ice usually does not accumulate quickly and we had the tools to fight it. The real problem in icing conditions is clear ice. This can build very fast, and can kill lift and quickly overweight the aircraft. Then immediate action is required. In my mind our conditions were manageable. Other aircraft were not reporting any major issues, just rime ice. Suddenly Gary turned to me and said we were going into Ottawa, let ATC know. Somewhat surprised, I picked up the mike and requested Ottawa as our destination.

After landing we secured the plane and found a ride to a small inn nearby. Gary called the company to explain our delay. During this time I wondered if all this is necessary. We grabbed some sleep and had dinner then back to the airfield. We filed the flight plan to Detroit and were airborne. With a normal flight with little conversation. Back home there were a few questions. I had mine but it did not matter. The captain calls the shots, my job is to assist the captain. (The feelings come out, and sometimes I fly sitting on my hands.)

Chapter Twenty-Five

The Other Wings of the Fleet

Flying at night is the same as flying in the day,
except you can't see.
　　　　　—Dave English, *Slipping the Surly Bonds*

The only time flying with Bentley that I flew someone of importance happened in the Cessna 402 N3255Q that was used mostly for passengers and small light freight. Different than the Beeches, they have tricycle landing gear, turbo-charged engines and cabin class. In early summer, 1977, I received a call to crew the flight for Senator Robert Griffin from Metro to West Branch, Michigan.

At the allotted time we taxied to the fixed base operator (FBO) at Metro, Page Airways to pick up our passenger. It was a short flight up north. Upon landing, Senator Griffin was met by a small group. He thanked us for the ride and then he was gone. It was an uneventful trip, but it stands out in my mind over many other trips.

I flew another memorable trip with Captain Bob McTavish. His full-time job was working for North Central Airlines on the ground, while building his flight time working for Bentley. He eventually was hired by Northwest as flight crew.

This flight in the 402 was just a short run to Youngstown, Ohio and back. The weather was good. I had flown with Bob only a few times before so we were kind of new to each other. He was a good captain and we exchanged flying duties regularly. This trip started normally enough. Bob was flying, I was doing the radios, and the non-flying pilot duties.

The tower instructed us to position and hold on runway 3C at Metro but soon we were cleared for takeoff. Not long after leaving the ground Bob called for gear up. I reached for the lever and raised the gear, but during the climb Bob seemed uncomfortable with the way the ship was flying. I could feel it too. As Bob reviewed the aircraft conditions, he found the gear not up. I was shocked, believing I had raised the gear handle. With the gear up and tucked under the airplane things smoothed out nicely.

Bob did some investigation, and realized I lifted the handle only to the center of the switch, not all the way to the up position. He reviewed the error with me, and how to make sure it will be prevented in future flights. This was just another lesson on the learning curve of aviation knowledge, the best kind because nobody hurt, nothing broken, just my pride, flying in the right seat.

Chapter Twenty-Six

Flying in the Freezer

You can land anywhere once.
—Dave English, *Slipping the Surly Bonds*

Everyone knows winter brings cold temperatures. Flying at altitude can bring extreme temperatures that can be life threating if not guarded. Producing heat in the cabin and cockpit in Beeches, was created by a gasoline-fired heater named a Janitroll. When they worked they would blow out plenty of heat. Pilots were able to fly in a short-sleeved shirt comfortable in the middle of winter. We would fire up the heater just before taxi or after takeoff. Most of the time they lit, if not, we returned for maintenance to inspect.

Safu and I did a trip in February 1977 to Oshawa, Canada (YUL), on a Friday night/Saturday morning. Climbing out of Oshawa, Safu engaged the start switch for the heater and got nothing. We requested from ATC permission to deviate from our course. They approved the request, we slowed things down, dropped the gear, added some flaps and still had no heat.

Now it was decision time. Do we go back to Oshawa? Our decision was unanimous to push on. We were both dressed for winter with boots, gloves, coats, hats and long johns; Safu preferred his wife's nylon panty hose. They worked well, too. As we labored to bring our destination closer, our bodies grew colder. We tried whatever we could to stay warm and preserve as much heat in our bodies but it wasn't working out. By the time we reached London, Ontario we could hardly move our hands and feet. Finally, we were handed off to Detroit approach control to sequence our landing there. On final approach we agreed to both stay on the controls for the landing. We taxied to the ramp, calling dispatch to help us exit the aircraft. In the office, it took time and assistance to remove our boots. Safu set his boots with his feet still inside on the radiator and melted part of the soles. With our outer clothing removed, we sat close to a heat radiator drinking coffee. We realized how serious our rush to get home can be. Lesson learned.

Chapter Twenty-Seven

The Call to Corporate

Fly it until the last piece stops moving.
—Dave English, *Slipping the Surly Bonds*

In late June 1977, something surprising happened. I received a call from Paul Lambarth, the FAA examiner who administered my commercial and instrument check rides. He owned the small flight school at Ann Arbor Airport. Paul had been told that I was building time flying Beeches out of Metro. Paul flew Corporate for many years in the fifties and sixties. All his time was corporate and instruction flying, teaching people to fly.

I must have made a good impression with him. He called to see if I would be interested in flying right seat with him on a Cessna 421 owned by Domino's Pizza. I told him first, that I wanted to run this by my boss at Bentley, Jim Ervine, to see if I could do both without too much conflict. Jim understood what an opportunity this would be for me.

This type of flying for the most part would be scheduled normally a week in advance. When I would be flying with them I could just block my time off with Bentley, adding me back on the schedule when I returned. All parties agreed, and I was elated.

Domino's purchased a Cessna 421, their first venture into a real cabin class twin, the N number 20GS. This was one of the first 421 models Cessna produced. She was equipped with state-of the-art-avionics, a flight director FD-108, Bendix weather radar, radar altimeter, King Radio package and hot windshield. This was all airline quality. The 421 truly had the look of a mini airliner with pressurized cabin, plush seating for six, beverage and snack bar, but no coffee maker, just two thermoses. I would be responsible to have coffee hot and ready for each flight out.

I knew flying with Paul was going to be a challenge. He was old school through and through. The 421 was certificated for single pilot IFR flight. However, Paul was so accustomed to the two-pilot flying that he wasn't going to change now. He wasn't getting any younger either and two sets of eyes, ears and hands, would be helpful and reassuring. My first trip with Domino's in the 421 was in late June, 1977, a short trip to Traverse City (TVC) and return to Willow Run, our home base. We did this trip back-to-back, as there were too many passengers for one trip. It was so refreshing to fly in nice clothes, and not get all greasy, I could get used to this.

For a while, flying sitting on my hands was the norm with Paul. He would act like I was not even on board at times, until he wanted something. I could fly with the best of them while feeling useless but reminding myself not to let this behavior get to me. Instead, I used time to really get to know 20GS, learning the cockpit layout, flight director operation, the circuit breaker panels and positions gave me lots to study.

We made flights to many east coast cities, making stops and dropping people off along the way. Then we'd turn around, pick them back up and head back to YIP. This made for long days for everyone, but made for good aircraft utilization. One of our most visited cities was Zanesville, Ohio. Zanesville was a large distribution center for Domino's and some company executives also lived there. Having to make that stop after a long return trip was at best trying, but whatever the company needed we tried our best to assist.

We flew our passengers to mainly eastern destinations—New York, Rhode Island, Ohio, Indiana, Kentucky, North Carolina, Virginia, Pennsylvania, and Tennessee, including Michigan.

N20GS was a first-generation Cessna 421 suffered from some shortcomings which included small fuel tanks, and external baggage.

Many of these upgrades were made in later models, making the 421 a much more comfortable and functional aircraft, for distance flying.

During the first trip I made with Mr. Tom Monaghan, founder and president of the company, I was somewhat on edge; big titles make me nervous, but was pleasantly surprised. He was very down-to-earth and easy going. At one of our stops we talked a bit and he told me of his enjoyment of flying. At one point he was working on his private pilot license.

We would often fly a group of home office people into a city, a company tactic used often. They would do a surprise inspection to check the operation of the franchisee. How was their store performing and how well were they following company guidelines. Domino's was big on standardization.

On a trip I will never forget, we were taxiing for takeoff at Cincinnati Lunken Airport in the afternoon and Mr. Monaghan went to the back to get a coffee. It was cold. I loaded two hot thermoses in the morning as normal. No one I can ever recall drank coffee in the afternoon. Mr. Monaghan relayed to Paul his disappointment. The next thing I knew we were cleared back to the terminal. Paul shut down the left engine, while I jumped out with the two thermoses, ran in to the restaurant and had them filled. Back on board I secured the door, loaded the coffee dispenser and poured Mr. Monaghan a hot coffee. It all worked out, although some could have called that dereliction of my duties. However, I was not asked for hot coffee in the afternoon and I never added hot coffee in the afternoon except when Mr. Monaghan was on board.

Chapter Twenty-Eight

Inside A Thunderstorm

*Oh, that I had wings like a dove, for then would I
fly away and be at rest.*

—Psalm 55:6

One of the most horrific flights I ever experienced happened on board 20GS. On a typical summer day in August, our route for the day was YIP-OSU-PKB-PKB-OSU-YIP, Willow Run, Columbus, Parkersburg, Columbus, and Willow Run. Most of these stops were short drop offs, quick turn arounds and back in the air with the exception of OSU, Columbus Ohio, State University Airport.

Our arrival in Columbus was late morning and our group said that they would return about two pm, for departure. We felt some big deal was beganing. Paul and I had 20GS fueled, checked all necessary items and waited for our passengers return. We ate some lunch while sitting in the pilots lounge at the fixed base operator (FBO) and observed the local weather radar. I could see the thunderstorms building off to our west near the Chicago area. If our passengers returned on time things would be fine.

The weather that afternoon was very hot and humid. The air was thick and couldn't wait to let loose its moisture content. Just walking to 20GS on the ramp and back I was covered in sweat. Two o'clock passed and no passengers arrived. We watched the line of thunderstorms building and moving east. We wanted to get back to YIP. There was no need to overnight this close to home. Three o'clock passed and no passengers. The sky west of Columbus was taking on that ominous look and feel. Paul was showing signs of frustration, but the quandary comes later once the passengers arrived whether to go or stay.

Finally our passengers showed. It must have been a good meeting. They all were feeling no pain. Paul made the decision to go, surprising to me. He felt we could stay low and pick our way through the cells with the radar. He had much more time working airborne weather radar than I. We loaded our four drunken passengers into the cabin, Paul fired up the engines as I secured the door. One of the passengers told me that they had just locked up one of the biggest deals ever for the company, their reason for celebration.

In the cockpit I received our clearance to YIP, taxi instructions and some changes to our route. Everything seemed okay. Surprisingly, it was not raining at the field on takeoff but visibility was low with haze. We reached our cruising altitude of four thousand feet, solidly on the gauges.

Things let loose, with rain beating against the airplane sounding like stones hitting the metal, not water droplets. My first thought, how can these engines ingest this much water and keep turning. It was incredible. Paul was flying but we were both glued to the radar screen. I also monitored the engine gauges, and the ride didn't feel too bad at this time. The rain was so heavy the cells were concealed in the radar picture which masked our plight. This uncertainty suggested that I latch down my lap belt. Then wham! The bottom literary fell out of the airplane. We are descending as if we are in an elevator. Paul yelled for me to get on the controls with him. Both of us pulled back on the yoke. The altimeter was still unwinding. How can this be? Every pilot knows you pull back, the airplane goes up, you push forward, and it goes down. Not so today. Our altitude was not very high to start and now we were moving closer to the ground. For the first time in my life, I was piloting an airplane and having no control. As quickly as we were shoved down, the direction changed and we were climbing uncontrollably. Air Traffic control (ATC) was trying to contact us. I grabbed the mike, told them too busy, can't talk and threw the mike down.

Paul looked at me and asked if he was bleeding. Turning his head so I could get a better view, I saw blood running down his left side forehead from a gash near his hair line. My first thought, you SOB, you got me into this mess, and you'd better not pass out on me now. Thinking somewhat more clearly I realized head wounds draw lots of blood, although not a judge of the wound severity. Paul showed no signs of passing out, just bewildered. He took his handkerchief and held it tightly against his forehead. Our elevator ride was still in full swing. By jockeying the throttles and control surfaces we were able to keep 20GS upright, engines running, and out of the ground. In these conditions, flying "attitude" is all you can fly; holding headings and altitude are impossible.

Almost as quickly as our near disaster began, the battle ended. We regained radio and radar contact with ATC. They re-routed us by way of Cleveland. Finally, up was up and down was down, gratefully. It's very difficult to say how long our ordeal lasted, time was suspended. My guess is maybe fifteen minutes. Those minutes seemed like hours or even days. It's hard to judge time in that state of mind. When processing so much information there was little room for anything else cluttering my mind.

The assessment was that we were flying in so much precipitation it prohibited our view of the storm cells on the radar screen, allowing us to penetrate a thunderstorm. We penetrated the storm at four thousand feet. Another factor that kept us alive. Thunderstorms in the Midwest normally don't extend to the ground, like the big ones out west. Had we been at an altitude of ten or fifteen thousand feet it could have been a completely different circumstance and outcome.

The remainder of our flight was quite smooth with very little talking, lots of reflection and even some sunshine approaching YIP. I had figured out how Paul cut his head. His seat belt was loose to start, and when we hit the first cell his body lifted up and into the speaker grille over his seat, hitting one of the screws.

Upon landing we taxied to the Butler ramp. Our hungover, starry-eyed passengers deplaned and headed for the parking lot with almost nothing said. Paul was playing the light hearted, no big deal role. I was left with the big job of putting the cabin back together. Cream and sugar packets, stir sticks, pop cans, mixers, booze bottles, snacks, ice cubes were all scattered like remnants of a tornado. This flight was my deepest "come to Jesus" moment. Failing to honor my promise to Him by not living a Christian life and having sin, Jesus was still there in my moment of need, As sure as the nose on my face I know that there was only one person guiding 20GS that day in the storm, and it wasn't Paul or me, it was God, absolutely, positively. The fear of the moment was enormous yet I felt inner peace, not being alone during this time of chaos. Once again His grace, His love has carried me. His strength, His power was overwhelming. Am I worthy of such grace?

Chapter Twenty-Nine

The Domino Fell

Dad, I left my heart up there.
— Francis Gary Powers, age fourteen

The trips with Domino's in 20GS continued at a normal pace. I also fit in as many Bentley trips in the Beech that my schedule could handle. This Monday morning trip started with usual departure preparation, making the coffee, filling the thermoses and driving to Willow Run. When I entered the Butler hangar I did not see 20GS. I walked over to one of the maintenance guys and asked where it was. He responded that some guys came in yesterday and flew it away. It was sold the day before. I could not believe my ears. I was angry and in shock.

There was only one way to get the real answer and that was to go to the home office on Yost Road and talk to Mr. Monaghan myself. There we exchanged greetings and I sat down. I explained to Mr. Monahan my encounter at the hangar. I asked him if it was true that 20GS was sold. His first reaction was, "Didn't Paul tell you?" He did apologize to me and began to tell me all the shortcomings 20GS had for the company and that this would not be the last airplane in Domino's future.

He confirmed that he liked me and my style. He even made an offer for me to stay with the company and run one of his pizza stores so I would be available when a new airplane came into the picture. However, I responded that I am a pilot and I want to fly airplanes. We shook hands, I left his office and never saw Mr. Monaghan again. I believe never to look back. Its history, cast in stone, reviewed, but never changed.

Chapter Thirty

The Cessna 421 Oddball

Learn from mistakes of others. You won't live long enough to make all of them yourself.
—Dave English, *Slipping the Surly Bonds*

I t wasn't long before I heard from Paul. I told him how upset I was about the 20GS story. He called to tell me he picked up a new job flying a 421-C model for a steel broker, Ewald Steel, out of Metro, and asked me to crew with him. As upset as I was about 20GS, I was ready for a new flying job.

Paul and I met at Page Airways to inspect our new aircraft, N500ES, much improved from 20GS with more baggage area outside, more fuel capacity, a nicer cabin layout, a real coffee pot, and newer avionics. We had the Page people pull her out of the hangar. After doing a thorough walk-around we entered the cockpit for some training. It was a nice clear day and off we went to do some maneuvers. One other big improvement very noticeable with 500ES was increased power.

Our first trip DTW-BMH-DTW Detroit, Birmingham, Alabama and back to Detroit we carried three passengers, the owner and two younger relatives. This may be the whole company. They traveled with, having little conversation. The trip to Birmingham

(BMH) was great; nonstop with plenty of fuel in reserve. The improvements to 500GS from 20GS were evident and pleasing.

This company's milk run was to Galion, Ohio. Other trips were to Alabama, Mississippi, Illinois, Pennsylvania, and Birmingham.

We never got close with our passengers like we did with Domino's. We felt more like a chauffeur service than anything else. So we moved on. This was the last time I flew with Paul. Even all his quirks and old-fashioned ways, he was a good man, a good mentor and a very good pilot.

Chapter Thirty-One

Bye Bye, Bentley

Don't judge those who try and fail. Judge only those who fail to try.

— H. Jackson Brown Jr.

Now my efforts returned to Bentley. With Jim Burns and his wife, Alisa, securing a small business loan, things changed. Different aircraft showed up and others left. Their small trucking company that operated out of the Metro office became more active. My time flying the Beech was more focused on my captain check ride. The responsibility of the flights handed to me allowed me to make captain decisions and it felt good; real learning.

Safu was also still flying for Bentley. We drew a trip to Oshawa together flying N 220WH. On our return home things became a little odd when dispatch diverted us to return to Willow Run. While picking up our freight there for another trip we were told not to return to Metro; strange but do-able. Upon arrival at YIP we taxied to Butler to refuel and load our freight. We instructed the line boy to top off our tanks, and went inside to do some paperwork. Then it dawned on us. We told the line boy to top us off. Our problem is 220WH has auxiliary out-board fuel tanks and the left one has no bladder in it. We rushed out on the ramp screaming at the kid to stop and a good thing he did. He did not put any fuel in the left tank missing the Bladder. However, he did fill the right auxiliary tank, so now we have an extra fifty gallons in the right wing.

During the loading we discussed our options and came to this conclusion. We have plenty of runway and were not over gross weight, or out of CG (center of gravity envelope); we'd make a nice slow acceleration and get the feel of the controls. Then do an easy climb out and then burn off the right aux tank first. The plan was implemented and all went well. Lesson learned. We could have averted this issue if we had covered the caps for the outboard auxiliary tanks with tape, marking as unusable.

Returning to Metro we were told the reason for our diversion. Creditors were at the office to take possession of N220WH. Things were getting real shaky at Bentley with pilots, mechanics, office staff, everyone but the owners. Their reaction was business as usual. My training for captain was progressing to the point I was ready to fly with the FAA.

Then it hit. Operations at Bentley stopped. It was over. Shutting down at this time couldn't have happened at a worse time for me. All the co-workers and friends, the airplanes, and places, all gone except the memories. Regrettably this will be a common theme in the on-demand air charter business.

Surprisingly, I got word of a small operator at Metro looking for captains, flying Beech 18s, a nose-wheel and a tri-gear aircraft. Not a lot of tri-gear Beeches were produced and not extremely popular as freighters. The company needed captains and I needed a check ride. With a little training and formalization I was at the FAA office ready to show my competence as captain, flying the Beech 18 for Inspector Neil Humphrey. On September 28, 1978, I became a licensed Beech 18 captain.

Most of my trips with them were single pilot, something I wasn't real comfortable with. I never felt comfortable flying the tri-gear Beech and making trips to Oshawa in it. With so many things not feeling good and too few feeling right, we parted company. I did have a little remorse about getting my captains ticket with them and leaving so soon. However, a man's got to do what he has to do.

Chapter Thirty-Two

Two Became Three

Treasure the love you receive above all. It will survive long after your gold and good health have vanished.
—Og Mandino

I was well into my flying career and living with two other pilots in a Westland townhouse when Detroit was blasted with a huge snow storm. Nothing moved in the city for three days, and my roommates and I were going stir crazy, cooped up at home. I received a call from an old friend Sue Riley inviting us to a party.

The roads were still bad, but we made our way to the party. Entering, we grabbed a beer and we started to mingle. The people were friendly and talkative. To my amazement sitting at a bar stool was Connie. A conversation began and we filled in the blanks from many years apart. We picked up our lives from Emerson Junior High. We talked the whole night, and when it was time to go we made plans to meet again. My roommates were kidding me on the way home that they better start looking for my replacement in the townhouse. I was told they could see the change in my eyes and face. How right they were.

Connie and Laura had an apartment in Westland, and Connie worked for Guardian Glass at their corporate office. I spent a lot of

146

time at her apartment getting to know Laura and the cat, Bandit. We watched TV and did things that didn't cost much.

Connie and I developed a strong bond quickly. Because of our past relationship we already knew a lot about each other and our families. We were spending almost all our free time together. On the days I was flying things were different. Getting home quickly became a bigger priority than ever before. Flying airplanes for a living was a dream of a lifetime well as having a serious relationship with the only girl I really loved. I knew where I wanted to go with our future. But I wondered if Connie was at the same place.

I gave a lot of thought about Laura and if the relationship were to develop, was I ready for instant family and all the responsibility that goes with it. I have always loved kids and if things were to advance I wanted to adopt Laura and be her dad. I was convinced I wanted to spend the rest of my life with Connie and Laura.

I was twenty five years old and ready to start a new life as a married man. But the only way to find out was to ask Connie to marry me.

Between flying jobs I tended bar at Salvatore's Italian Restaurant. John Salvatore was a friend of mine and my brother Tom, from the old neighborhood. He ran the bar at his family restaurant, and taught me the trade. The layout in the lounge had secluded booths and the strolling musicians, would be perfect for my plan. I knew the musicians well and told them of my plan to ask Connie to marry me on April fool's Day (only a coincidence). They came over to our booth after dinner and played "What Are You Doing the Rest of Your Life." It all went off well and Connie said she would marry me.

We married August 11, 1978, at Augsburg Lutheran in Redford. Connie was more beautiful than ever, escorted by her dad, a very distinguished former Marine. The ceremony was quick and in the eyes of the Lord, family and friends we were made one. Then we had our reception at Roma's Hall in Garden City. Family and friends were a big help. The reception was great fun. In every wedding there is something that goes wrong and we were no exception. We were sitting at the head table not far from the cake, and I just happened to catch some movement at the cake table, as it fell over.

Leaving the hall we were invited to Bill Ramsey's house to continue the celebration, which we did. Finally, we arrived at our hotel room about three am. We had a bag full of cards that we could not wait to open so we started reading. The next day we went to my dad's to visit with the out-of-town families. From our gift of money we able to pay Dad what we had borrowed from him. He was trying to push it back to me. He had done so much and we loved him for it.

My brother Tom loaned us his MG convertible and we were off to Traverse City. We secured a room on the top floor of the downtown Park Place Hotel, with a great view of the water. We dined at the hotel restaurant, Top of the Park. Our meal of Chateaubriand was served table side and a new experience for Connie and me. In the morning we headed to the town of Northport, then continued along the Lake Michigan side of the peninsula. We found Leland, a small resort town with lots of charm. We stumbled upon the Falling Waters Motel and decided to check in. The view from our room overlooked Lake Leelanau and flowed into Lake Michigan. We ate at the upscale restaurant, The Cove. We liked the area so well we extended our stay and had breakfast at the little diner named The Bluebird. We were impressed by the simplicity and quality. Our journey continued down Highway 22 out of Leland to Sleeping Bear Dunes, Frankfort and Arcadia, just a beautiful drive. We sensed our fantasy trip coming to an end and reality of life as a family entered into our thoughts.

Wedding day

Chapter Thirty-Three

Building a Company

There is never a wrong time to do the right thing.
—Dad

Where do I go from here? I felt the need to use my experience and good common sense acquired in the air charter business. After investigating aircraft that would be suited for the on-demand automotive air charter business my analyses showed four promising picks. The one that stuck in my mind and the one I always came back to was the Short Brothers and Harland SC-7 Skyvan, built in Belfast, Northern Ireland.

Production began in the early sixties, powered first by an Astazou engine that did not perform well. Changes to the power plant were made and a Garrett Air Research Turbine TPE-331 was installed. This was the missing link. Now the aircraft performed superbly. Able to operate in and out of unimproved short field strips, and with a large rear-door loading area made for a perfect match with the improved engine.

Exploring further, I found an airline operating on the east coast flying Skyvans transporting scheduled freight. I contacted Summit Airlines in Philadelphia for more information. To my surprise they informed me that their Skyvans were being replaced with Convair

580s and the Skyvan fleet was for sale through Great Planes Sales in Tulsa. Amazing how this all began falling into place.

Making contact with Great Planes Sales, I was referred to Mr. Gary Conklin. Gary knew the Summit fleet well; it was his job to sell them. At this point all I needed was a price, so I could continue assembling the numbers for my plan. The most desirable ships were in the five-hundred to five hundred fifty thousand dollar range.

I knew now the Skyvan was the one. Bringing this airplane into the automotive assembly market will fill a void and possibility even create a new market. The biggest selling point was the rear door opening large enough to load a pallet. With a rugged fixed gear and high wing, it resembles a flying UPS truck. Short field takeoff and landing, and the ability to access smaller, close-in airports helped to accommodate our customers. Not pretty, but a real work horse.

Now the million dollar question, could I find financing and a partner. Somehow I discovered a packaging company, WoodFab, located in Dearborn, Michigan looking at expanding its business. Working this lead, I secured an appointment with the president of the company, Jerry Joseph. He was the son of the founder of WoodFab, Jack Joseph, and seemed very open to my plan. Jerry added Jim Lawson Woodfab's CFO to our discussion group. Jim Lawson. Jim had a very intelligent business mind. They both liked the air charter concept and the Skyvan.

With Jim Lawson's business mind and my air charter concept, a business plan was assembled. The plan was proposed to our financial company, GE Capital and financing for the Skyvan was secured.

Securing an operating certificate from the FAA became the next hurdle. People would need to be hired, but only the most key members. With no revenue, the expenses needed to be kept minimal. My first employee was Dave Brunsguarrd, an old Bentley Captain, good pilot and easy going personality. Dave would be our chief pilot and trainer. Our Certificate of Application to the FAA would take place during their rewriting of the complete Part 135 Air Charter operation regulations. These regulations pertain to smaller aircraft, less than nineteen passengers. Scheduled airlines are governed by Part 121 FAA regulations.

Operating under and using for pilot training an existing 135 certificate would make for an easier transition with the FAA, instead of all new certification procedures like pilot training would be a transfer from one certificate to the other, allowing us time to create the new company manuals under the new FAA program.

In locating an existing certificate to use, I contacted Jim Timoszyk, my old flight school owner. I explained to Jim our plan, and he was in agreement, adding compensation for him and the right for his company to do the Skyvan's maintenance when purchased. Brunsy and I completed check rides on Timoszyk's 135 certificate, in a Cessna-172, making the transfer legal, while working feverishly on the operations, training, and maintenance manuals for our new certificate. Things were coming together. Now it was time for Skyvan training at Summit Airlines for Brunsy and me. We were close to taking delivery of our new Skyvan N50DA from Great Planes sales.

We flew to Philadelphia for three days of Skyvan ground and flight training. Our trainer, Jim Scott was a senior pilot for Summit. The training went great and on time. The company was getting to the point where we needed to put a name to this operation. A few thoughts were tossed around and the one that stuck was Skyhawk Air Services, with all in agreement. Now the vision had a name.

Returning from PHL it was time for the final details to take ownership of the Skyvan. Gary Conklin flew up in an MU-2 from Tulsa. We closed the deal of just over a half million dollars. Gary flew Brunsy and me back to Tulsa to fly home to Detroit our new airplane, N50DA. Our flight home was uneventful. It is easy to be comfortable in the roomy cockpit of the Skyvan with the entrance doors and aisles on both sides of the cockpit. What a change from the Beech 18s. The flight characteristics were both comfortable and forgiving. Arrangements were made to base the plane with Page Airways at Metro for now. Later we found a hangar close by Page for a decent price with lots of room.

The push was on for us to have our new operating certificate approved with the FAA. The First step is to have all manuals stamped and approved page by page. We purchased a generic manual and used it for our guide, making all the necessary changes and corrections to meet our needs. With great effort the operations, training, and maintenance manuals were ready. The final typing done. I am proud to say that Skyhawk was the first operator to be approved under the new FAA Part 135 Air Charter operations regulations by the Willow Run office. Finally with training complete and the pilots' six-month competency checks, we were a real Air Charter company. This process was repeated in Canada for our Canadian license also.

It did not take long before customers were calling our phone. We kept our automotive assembly customers in the loop with the desire to accommodate their needs, and were off to a good start, with trips to familiar towns, like Oshawa, Toronto, Indianapolis, Youngstown, and Dayton.

Skyvan Skyhawk air

Chapter Thirty-Four

JFK the Black Hole

The probability of survival is equal to the angle of arrival.

—Anonymous

A call came to us from a company that manufactures bullet-proof glass. They had utilized the Skyvan in the past with Summit Airlines, and were in need of our service. The plan was for us to pick up their load at JFK (my first trip there) then fly to Nacogdoches, Texas the destination. A motor-home company making a coach for one of the shahs in the Middle East had requested bullet-proof glass for it. This would be our cargo and the order was time sensitive. We needed to be airborne as soon as possible. The flight crew was Brunsy and me, and I would fly the first leg to JFK.

JFK was everything I had heard that it was. Flying at night and on instruments added to the interesting arrival. I must have upset one of our controllers, because he directed us over the ocean into the black hole of airspace for the longest time before turning us on the approach to JFK.

After landing we were directed to our pick up point to load cargo. The taxi instructions from the ground controller were rough and not overly helpful. We found our spot and shut down. This freight was heavy and needed extra care in loading. As we walked out to 50DA the person in charge of the freight approached me, put out his hand to shake. He reminded me how important it was for us to deliver on time. I assured him it would be done. While shaking hands he gave me the biggest tip I ever received—a hundred dollar bill! It was close to Christmas and this would come in handy. I felt it only right to tell Brunsy and split it with him. It was an uplifting surprise.

We entered 50DA, bringing her to life with our special cargo securely on board. Our course took us right down the eastern seaboard, passing Philadelphia, Atlantic City, Salisbury, and Norfolk. The sight amazed me. It looked like one huge city of lights that went on forever, without knowing where one city started and another stopped. The brightness seemed like daylight.

I was resting when interrupted by the frightening sound of an engine shutting down. Regaining my thoughts I asked Brunsy what was happening. He shut down one engine to save fuel. Now I was really puzzled. He went on to tell me that he had passed up my planned fuel stop because he figured we could make the trip in one fuel stop. I was shocked! He picked Tri-Cities Regional Airport serving the towns of Bristol, Kingston and Johnson, Tennessee (TRI) smack dab in the Cumberland Mountain's for our first stop, if we made it.

I located our position, still a distance from TRI. It was pitch black in the middle of the night, in unfamiliar terrain and we didn't know if we had enough fuel to make the airport. What a distressing sensation Brunsy's plan was to fire up the shutdown engine when we got close to the airport and make the landing on two engines. The last part of this leg was frightening, knowing from our charts we were in mountainous terrain, but no visual reference, will the shut-down engine restart? Once again fate played into our need, my guardian angel was present. We made the airport and landed safely on two engines. After shutting down we walked over to the office, to where the best part of this fiasco began. The FBO didn't open until seven am and they were the only fuel on the field. My biggest concern was meeting our customer in Nacogdoches on time. The clock finally showed 7:00 a.m. We topped off and headed west, with me flying.

How we made the connection with our customer on time I'm not sure, but the transfer went fine. After unloading we were off, heading for home. A new portable oxygen system had been installed into 50DA. We decided to take her up to eighteen thousand feet altitude and try it. The fuel flow to the engines was greatly reduced, saving considerable fuel, a noteworthy way to finish a fuel-starved trip.

Chapter Thirty-Five

One-Way Passengers

If at first you don't succeed, well so much for skydiving.

—Henny Youngman

The versatility of the Skyvan fulfilled our needs in many different ways. I received a call from a skydiving club official inquiring if our airplane was available for rent to drop skydivers on weekends. He went on to explain that his club, the Herd, out of Pottstown, Pennsylvania utilized the Summit Skyvans on weekends in the past. Everyone fell in love with the plane, and it was missed. He assured me there were plenty of people wanting to jump out of a Skyvan and could fill the plane for a weekend.

We agreed the ferry time to Pottstown and back was our expense. Crew rooms and meals would be covered by the club. The Herd was quite savvy. They marketed the event as the Skyvan Boggy. People came from all around the area to jump out of the Skyvan. The big appeal was the rear exiting door. When skydivers exit an aircraft it's normally one at a time. With the Skyvan they can jump multiple people at once, known as mass exit.

Upon our arrival in Pottstown the airport was alive, much like the atmosphere at a county fair. The Herd had everything in place, from the people taking the money and organizing the loads (we set up for twenty people per load) to crowd control, food vendors, and even a souvenir stand. This was a big deal for these people. We were the rock stars.

In getting FAA approval for this "boggy," they required that we install ten-thousand-pound cargo straps across the floor and attach them to the cargo rings in the floor because we had no seat belts. This allowed the passengers to sit on the floor with their bodies under the strap, like a big seat belt. This worked out well for the FAA, though I never saw passengers use them.

Our first group ready and loaded, we were off to fourteen thousand feet. It does take a bit of time to reach that altitude. At altitude the signal to jump was announced, and within seconds our plane was empty. We learned that as people leave the aircraft rather quickly it is necessary to apply steady forward pressure on the yoke to compensate for the quick weight change. Then it's nose over, and back to the ground quickly. One of the great things about turbine engines is the ability to pull off the power to descend quickly without endangering the engines.

The Herd was a different bunch of people, super nice and accommodating. They just loved to jump out of airplanes, almost to an obsession. They sure were happy to have the "van" back, their nickname for the Skyvan. The loads kept on coming throughout the day in a very orderly manner. With the last load done, we were too. It was a lot of flying. The Herd invited us to their BBQ and bonfire later that night. The food was good and the booze was flowing. We made conversation with the people and truly enjoyed their company. Again we were given rock star status. Freighter pilots don't get treated like this so we ate it up. The next day we were informed that a record attempt was planned with twenty-five jumpers invited to exit at fifteen thousand feet, all trying to connect in flight. The trick to this jump is to deplane everyone quickly. This will allow maximum time in free fall to form up. At fifteen thousand feet they were out. Sadly their attempt did not materialize.

I did have a spiritual moment with the Herd, and that happened on the ground. Overall, the weekend went well, except for one glitch. After landing we taxied to our regular loading area. We kept the regular procedure of keeping the engines running due to the time factor and wear and tear on the engines, with all passenger loading from the rear.

During one of the flights on Sunday, we were thirsty and radioed down to see if we could get a couple of cold drinks for the pilots on our next stop. The reply came back, "You got it." Our load was released, and down we came. After landing, we taxied to our regular loading area. With the engines running. The gal came out of the office smiling with our drinks and headed directly to the front of the plane. She had no idea the propellers were turning. I motioned to her. I was so afraid she'd just walk into one. I frantically began waving my arms and yelling with the nastiest look I could make. Suddenly, ten feet from the propellers she looked upset, turned and walked away. This was nothing short of a miracle. Thank you Jesus.

Now, other than the drink incident this trip went great. The weather was wonderful and we worked with nice people. And we had a new way to generate revenue with the Skyvan.

After everything was said and done we headed for home. The Monday morning quarterbacking from the company was positive. We added some cash to the account and nothing broke, all good signs.

Now it was time to resume flying car parts and stay busy. Our customer calls kept coming in. My time was focused more on the position of Director of Operations than flying the line. I enjoyed everything about Skyhawk Air Services. Starting an air service with all the challenges and hurdles overwhelmed me at times, but flying the Skyvan was a joy. I knew something much greater than me was guiding this.

last man out

Chapter Thirty-Six

Real Skydivers

Challenges can be stepping stones or stumbling blocks. It's just a matter of how to view them.

—Anonymous

I received a call from the United States Parachuting Association inquiring about the Skyvan and its availability. The world championships were to be held in France this year. The French had chosen a rear exiting aircraft to be utilized (the host country's choice).

Most countries competing had very little experience jumping from a rear exiting aircraft. They were in a desperate way and needed help. The championship was just two months away. They needed the Skyvan for two weeks and would be willing to come to Michigan. Conferring with our people, we were able to assemble a plan. Our freight business was mainly at night; the USPA only needed daytime usage. Our only real concern was that the Skyvan must stay close to Detroit.

I called the USPA in Washington to lay out our plan. They loved the news. In hopes we would be receptive to their request, they arranged to use Tecumseh, Michigan, Meyer's field for their base of operations. This was home to an established and popular skydiving operation in Michigan. The airport southwest of Detroit, has a north-south 2,600-foot hard-surface runway suitable for the Skyvan. The USPA (team Mirror Image) enlisted the Canadian and British teams to join the training, to help offset expenses.

On the first day we assembled for an initial briefing I was overly impressed with the professionalism of all these people. The groups were made up of two and four-man teams. All teams jumped with a cameraman who recorded the complete jump. After each jump the team assembled at a room in the hangar to review the jump video, noting everyone's movement, position and landing on the designated target. They never missed!

On weekends the team practice took a pause. However the local jumpers flocked to the field and kept us busy. During the last local jump day, Sunday, the weather became an issue. I was on the ground working operations, and monitoring the radio traffic to our west. Pilots reported thunderstorms and I visually could see the changes to the west. It was getting close to shutting down operations. As the Skyvan landed there was another load ready to go. Speaking to the crew by radio, they commented that they could get this load in before the weather. The jumpers exited early, before ten thousand feet, because of the weather. The crew landed just before things got serious.

There were only a few jumpers from that load who made it back to the field. People were concerned and ground searches were organized. Fortunately all missing jumpers were found safe, some miles from the airport. A few reported ascending during their jumps. One main chute was lost but the jumper went to his reserve chute and landed safely. Once again Mother Nature played into my life in a disturbing way. Lives were saved but not by our actions, another strength was in power.

I am proud to say that after training the US team, Mirror Image went on to win the 1979 world championships in France. They beat the French on their home turf, in their aircraft. Skyhawk Air Services participation in training was noted in the USPA magazine.

Chapter Thirty-Seven

New Look, New Direction

Regardless of what company you work for, never forget the most important product you're selling is yourself.

—Dad

Our company business was in operation during the sky-dive training and freight trips resumed at the normal pace. With income flowing, the home office concluded it's time to have 50DA painted. When purchased her color was all white, void of any Summit Airlines markings. Searching for a paint shop lead me to Kal Aero in Kalamazoo, Michigan. Surprisingly, I found a connection there. Jim Ervin my former chief pilot with Bentley Flight Service was now chief pilot for Kal Aero.

Jim fixed me up with their paint shop supervisor. With only a rough sketch submitted, their team took the idea and ran with it. Within a few days a final draft was submitted. It looked great. A date was set with Kal Aero to bring 50DA in for one week of work. Kal Aero was true to their word. One week later we picked up 50DA. What a change! That plain-looking, white UPS truck with wings now had character.

The paint graphic entailed the head of a hawk starting at the plane's nose then flowing back along the full side, then flaring up to the tail in blue with red accent stripes. The word Skyhawk in block letters made an impressive vision. The wow factor was accomplished. Now she's a piece of art.

Even as beautiful as 50DA looked with a new paint job it wasn't enough to increase business and counter a slowing economy. Car sales in 1980 were starting to slow with less calls from the assembly plants for charters. This change started slowly but increased swiftly. With less charters a new avenue of revenue was needed. The $9,800-a-month payment for 50DA was crippling.

I put together a classified ad to run in newspapers and trade publications around the country to sell our services—trying to hook anything to keep us flying. Once again fate came into play. I received a call from Rod Thompson of Anchorage, Alaska. He had a need for a Skyvan, and wanted to fly down to discuss a possible arrangement.

I picked up our visitor at Metro and returned to the home office. Rod Thompson, representing Bush Air of Bethel, Alaska was our guest. Rod, a retired Air Force Officer, lived in Anchorage, and commuted to Bethel, five hundred miles east of Anchorage. He explained that business in Alaska was very unique. Flying is a necessity to their way of life in Alaska. There are lots of work contracts with BLM (Bureau of Land Management) the USPS (United States Postal Service) and many others. Rod was very familiar with the Skyvan, noting that almost all Skyvans in the US are operating in Alaska.

An agreement was made with Rod's company that they would pay us $20,000-a-month lease for the use of 50DA. We would supply two crews. Bush Air would pay for crew expenses in Alaska, and Skyhawk would pay expenses for ferrying the Skyvan to Alaska commuting crews to Detroit/Anchorage would be split by both companies. This was a business agreement without a contract, on good faith only. Maybe not the best setup, but it created instant income and kept us working.

Chapter Thirty-Eight

North to Alaska

Three things kill pilots in Alaska, weather, weather, weather.
> —Don Woodward Jr., veteran bush pilot
> *Flying* magazine, September 1966

The date was set to ferry 50DA to Anchorage on March 17, 1980, St. Patrick's Day. The rain poured as we loaded our personal gear into 50DA, along with a survival kit I assembled. Flying as I knew it was about to change in a way I had only imagined. Having knowledge from backpacking in remote areas was reassuring for me while setting out on a journey into wilderness of this enormous proportion. Saying goodbye to my wife, Connie, hurt, knowing she carried the burden of taking care of the home front, our daughter, and her full-time job. I'm departing on a great encounter that I've dreamed about for many years.

Our plan is to be in Anchorage by the next evening. The crew for the ferry flight was me and Joe Puggarella, a good pilot with lots of flying time. We closed up the Skyvan and headed to our first stop, Thunder Bay, Ontario our port of entry into Canada. Customs performed their normal inspection; however, they interrogated me about the shotgun on board. I explained that it was only for emergency survival purposes and would stay in the aircraft. Knowing that Alaska was our destination, and we were just transiting Canada, entry was permitted.

With a fresh load of jet fuel, we were airborne; next stops Winnipeg, Manitoba then on to Saskatoon, and Saskatchewan. Finally calling it a day in Edmonton, Alberta.

Day two brought clouds, rain and low visibility. Our thoughts on having an excellent view of the Canadian Rockies were crushed. The route of flight would take us to Dawson Creek, British Columbia, Whitehorse, and the Yukon Territory, arriving back in the United States at Northway, Alaska, then completing our day flying into Anchorage. The trip from Edmonton to Whitehorse was discouraging, IFR (instrument flight rules) on the gauges most of the flight. But our luck did change departing Whitehorse.

The overcast lifted by the time we reached Northway. The weather was CAVU (ceiling and visibility unlimited). This allowed the last leg into Anchorage over the Alaskan range to be breathtaking. We could see into tomorrow. Radio reports broadcasted visibility fifty miles plus, unheard of down below. With Joe at the controls, I moved from side to side in the cockpit capturing pictures, consuming a full roll of film. The city boy has found the mountains.

In Anchorage there were many things needed to be accomplished before we headed to Bethel. There was ground school, learning a new company manual, and orientation on Alaska flying. The Skyvan also needed to be reworked and inspected. The most significant change included adjusting torque settings on the engines. Normal settings had been twenty pounds in full reverse, now it's fifty; necessary for flying in the bush. The training took place in a second floor hangar at Anchorage International Airport. In three days Joe, two other pilots with Bush Air and I knocked out all the book work. The time spent was both educational and enjoyable. We're ready for Bethel. Anchorage resembled "any town" USA. Other than the mountains and the ocean, it fit fine in Michigan.

One morning, from the doorway of the hangar on the second floor, I noticed an impressive view on the horizon. I questioned my classmate, Tim, and to my amazement, he replied, "That's Mt.

McKinley." I was astonished viewing a mountain that was almost three hundred miles away! That's like standing in Detroit and seeing the Mackinaw Bridge.

Tim a new hire to Bush Air recently returned from Guam where he had been flying for three years. He needed to get his Toyota pickup to Bethel. We checked the dimensions and weight, and decided to fly it out in the Skyvan. I had carried some unusual cargo, but never a whole truck! With the help of the company mechanic, Jim Wheeler, we loaded the truck. Besides, Joe me and Jim, there was Tim and his two adopted sons. The kids buckled up in the passenger compartment in the truck. This cargo setup was notable. I had flown many different auto parts and seen photos of complete vehicles being transported in developing nations around the world in the Skyvan. This was the beginning of my unique Alaska flying adventure.

Chapter Thirty-Nine

Flying the Bush

Trust your captain.... But keep your seatbelt securely fastened.

—Anonymous

We departed Anchorage airport, a unique place with not only a major international airport, but also a large seaplane base on Lake Hood. All traffic from the lake is controlled by Anchorage Tower making traffic very chaotic at times.

We stopped for fuel in McGrath, my first bush town. Government style buildings were numerous. We topped off the tanks, and headed to Bethel.

After crossing the Kuskokwim Mountains, the tundra was dreary and flat with many small frozen lakes. We followed the Kuskokwim River into Bethel. After landing on a modern day, hard surface runway we taxied to the Bush Air hangar and began the unloading process.

Bethel was the hub of transportation for the bush villages in this region. Wein Air Alaska flies Boeing 737 "combies" into Bethel on a regular schedule from Anchorage. This Boeing is a very unique aircraft. The cabin is separated into two sections, front for freight, and rear for passengers with a movable bulkhead between them that allows the load to be arranged to accommodate the needs of the trip. A perfect setup for commercial airlines in the bush.

When people think of mail delivery they think of letters, cards, and small packages. In Alaska the mail means just about anything. People buy groceries, booze, tools,-anything that will fit into an airplane.

Once the freight arrives from Anchorage it's divided up in Bethel. Our job was to make final delivery of these items to the smaller villages around the area. This is just another demonstration of the many purposes the airplane provided to the Alaskan people.

Bethel's layout is simple, one road layout with the airport on one end, the garbage dump on the other. About midway, a side road links it all to the village and the river. A prominent feature and great land mark in Bethel was the large radar antennas resembling drive-in movie screens, left over from the Cold War DEW line (distant early warning), a project from the fifties, supposedly abandoned. The question I always had living in Bethel, why were there always vehicles in the parking lot?

Word came to us that 50DA was being outfitted for another purpose and our first job in the bush. We would be flying four hundred and fifty gallons of aviation fuel to Quinhagak, a native village on the Bearing Sea, one hundred miles south of Bethel. Multiple trips would be needed, with thousands of gallons to be delivered eventually. The village power generators were extremely low on fuel, due to poor planning and the harsh winter.

The company installed a 450-ferry tank out of a Havilland Caribou into the Skyvan. This would carry the needed fuel. Fuel trucks would fill the ferry tank in Bethel, like any another load. The flight to Quinhagak would be less than an hour. Landing would be made on a twelve hundred foot gravel strip. With strong winds along the coast this was not the greatest scenario, however I was told it would work.

These first trips were to be training for Joe and me. The flying was fine, but the cargo concerned both of us. So much so that Joe wanted nothing to do with this trip or any other trips in Alaska. He wanted a ticket home. Joe performed best in a structured, scheduled airline environment not remote, on demand cargo, especially hauling fuel. Now on my own, the fuel ferrying started. I must say I was nervous, but willing, still living my dream.

I was paired with a captain holding lots of bush flying and Skyvan time. His training would be perfect for my level of experience. I realized many pilots flying the Bush in Alaska carried credentials flying in Southeast Asia during the Vietnam War for Air America (the CIA Airline). They were great pilots, with amazing skills, but very loose with procedures including check-lists. Trying to blend into the flying regiment in the lower forty-eight would never work out for them. It would have been their demise.

The ferry tank filled and weather good, we were off to Quinhagak. The airport came into view a long way out, situated along the coast of Kuskokwim Bay in the Bearing Sea. The captain called for an abbreviated check-list turning on to final approach. The tiny gravel runway looked chilling, although there were no obstacles at either end of-the only beneficial detail to this scenario. The Captain planted the main wheels firmly on the approach end of the runway then rapidly transferred power into full reverse, forcefully throwing my body into my shoulder harness. Now I understand the necessity to change reverse torque settings in Anchorage; the stopping force was incredible. We came to rest with a piece of runway still ahead of us-what an adrenaline-charged sensation.

Taxiing to the drop off area I spotted four native men arranging fifty-five gallon drums. Their job was to transfer the payload of fuel. We used a small gas-powered pump to fill the drums from our large tank in the Skyvan (a dangerous procedure). The natives then hauled the drums to the village three quarters of a mile away to fill their generator tanks. This process was not fast, and also boring for the pilots. All we wanted to do was get back to Bethel and start the drill again. This was just the beginning of numerous trips to Quinhagak.

As the fuel trips continued, my emotions emerged. I could really die doing this. The odds were unusually high, and my nerves were put on trial. These thoughts weighed heavily on my mind, almost overwhelming me. Finally, I reached the conclusion that I call it quits and go back home or I conquer my fears and continue flying in Alaska.

The choice tried my soul. If we did crash with all this fuel on board, I wouldn't feel a thing; no suffering, no pain, just instant death. Placing my fears at the back of my mind, opened the capacity to appreciate this unique flying experience, and progress forward in peace.

The fuel resupply to Quinhagak lasted about a week. Within that time I accomplished my first bush landing. On the approach it's necessary to observe the runway touch-down spot, not scan the instrument panel. Eyes needed to be only on airspeed, with the power levers in one hand, the wheel in the other, and feet on the rudder pedals. Body and machine become fused with all the input from your brain. Not knowing entirely if the landing will be successful, or it will be necessary to abort and go around again was a constant consideration. This battle ends abruptly when the force of the wheels strike the ground, then power levers move to full reverse, catapulting us into our shoulder harnesses with rudders maintaining directional control. Finally, the plane comes to a stop. All this mind, power and energy focused on one purpose is a thrill like nothing experienced anywhere in my life.

Life in Bethel was surprisingly comfortable considering the location. I purchased some of the best fruits and vegetables of my life there, but also at the highest prices. Milk cost $5 a gallon, bread over $3.50 a loaf. Fortunately, the bill was paid from the company account with the store. There was even a fast food restaurant named Mac Swanson's. The burgers were six bucks. I compared them in taste and size to any quality burger around. The name, Mac Swanson for the burger joint was fitting. Mr. Swanson owned most of Bethel. In addition to the restaurant, he owned the hardware store, the grocery store, and marina.

Bethel was a dry town. I was told that the reason was years ago when drinking was legal it got out of control. The citizens were planning to shoot the mayor, and a riot was in the making. The Alaska State Troopers had to be flown in to regain control. At that point alcohol was banned. Even now booze was a real problem. People order their alcohol in Anchorage and the Weeney bird (the bush nickname for Wein Air Alaska's Boring 737s) flies it out to them. It's not illegal to drink in a residence, just in public.

Spring in the bush is a pleasant time. Everyone knows the dark days of winter are ending, the warm sunlit days are coming. The people of Bethel make up a lottery to pick the time when the ice in the river will leave, called "break up," allowing the river to flow again.

As long as the weather was good the flying continued. We transported cargo, mail and other supplies all around Bethel, visiting places like Aniak, Russian Mission, Kalskag, Holy Cross, Pilot Station, Shageluk, and Unalakleet.

Our routine on landing at the villages was to make a low pass over the village to let people know of our arrival, then swing into the pattern for landing. By the time we made the landing and taxied in, the locals were walking our way. This was a big event for them, something new. What's on board? And they were always helpful with the unloading process. During these times I liked to take photos to document my time there. Something I learned about the natives, they do not like to have their pictures taken. Whenever they spotted my camera pointed in their direction, they turned away. I was later told that they feel when their picture is taken, so was there soul. My photo taking became more discrete.

Cargo was always a surprise, as we never knew what was coming next. One morning arriving at the field, we noticed a panel truck parked next to the Skyvan. Its load contained heavy duty steel garbage cans (the same style used at military bases) that looked like they would last years. Our instructions were to deliver them to the village of Shageluk for the Bureau of Land Management (BLM).

The loading process began by laying the cans sideways, two rolls to the roof, into the Skyvan, and ending at the rear door opening. After securing two cargo straps over the load we were ready. Airborne, the conversation between the crew consisted of what the villagers would think of this load. Arriving at Shageluk, the locals approached to inspect the latest shipment. We opened the rear cargo door exposing the cans and began removing the cargo straps. They were puzzled. "What's this?" one said. We replied, "Garbage cans." All of them had a strange look on their faces. After wandering around the plane for a moment with no clue what this was, they began to walk back to the village.

Our job was to deliver the cargo to the village. So the three of us kicked the cans onto the tundra, buttoned up 50DA and headed for home. We had a good laugh all the way back, wondering which bureaucrat came up with the idea to send garbage cans to people who have never seen one and have no idea what they are used for. We returned to Shagelak a few weeks later and to our surprise the garbage cans were being used as fish containers. The locals used them to transport their fish. The natives were ingenious in many ways.

Generally their children do their schooling in the lower forty-eight states. But the Alaska government appropriated funds to build schools in the bush. Building schools here means building power stations, heating systems, dormitories for staff, etc. Foundations for structures must be built on pilings, like telephone poles inserted into the tundra, leaving part above ground. These poles must also be refrigerated to ensure no shifting with the changing conditions. After all the preparations, then it is time to ring the school bell. The air crews needed to use their imagination to construct a plan for moving the incredible amount of supplies for building a school. Someone had the idea to air drop supplies, in place of landing and unloading. This would save lots of time. Lumber was loaded in the Skyvan, then dropped over the closest lake to the building sight by flying low and slow with a slightly nose-up attitude. The boards were pushed out landing on the water. Then crews in boats retrieved the payload. Unfortunately when the boards hit the water they shattered on impact. The only thing accomplished was that we made a lot of tooth picks. Landings on the tundra would work fine.

As the flying continued my fear of meeting my Maker in the bush lessened, although the thought of mechanical breakdown, and being stuck with no help remained, but concern was quelled by our third crewmember, Jim Wheeler, our flight engineer. Jim had years of experience in Alaska, wrenching on aircraft. He knew the Skyvan and its engines extremely well. What set Jim apart was his extensive knowledge of airplanes. Years of tinkering, trouble shooting, and his MacGyver ability in the Alaskan environment made him extraordinary in my mind. He flew with us all the time. I can still vividly see him standing in the cargo area between the pilot's seats, wearing no ear protection. He was a godsend to us. No other crews were blessed with such a crewmember. With Jim on board my anxieties diminished.

While flying in Alaska I noticed that pilots were treated as special, a feeling I never felt in the lower forty-eight. The locals knew we flew the mail and carried most supplies to the villages and they were grateful. This was more than just meeting time schedules and making profits. Never did I feel this way flying car parts down below. I enjoyed it here in Alaska. Bethel enhanced my life more than any other town that I have been associated with. The dissimilarity in culture, housing, transportation and the ordinary way of life agreed with me.

Distance has always been an issue in the Alaska bush. A way of communication I found to be unique and functional was the "tundra drums." This was a program used in conjunction with the local AM radio stations where time was allotted for the locals to leave messages to family and friends when away from home. These were simply messages like "This is Bob Tulisk, Mom and Dad. I will be home tomorrow on the mail plane from Anvik." Simple but effective, these messages were made every hour all day, making use of the resources available to communicate in remote areas.

Of all my flights in Alaska the closest I came to Russia happened on a trip to Unalakleet. This village was located on Norton Sound roughly two hundred miles north of Bethel and two hundred miles from Russia (close enough for me). This village with a well-equipped airport for the bush was about the same size as Bethel, located on the shore of the Bearing Sea. Wein Air Alaska operates a B-737 daily from Anchorage. The village had a different look, a little more organized and less cluttered. The population of mixed Eskimo and Indian looked happier and more at ease. The ambience changed from village to village that I visited, a connection I took pleasure in. Unalakleet was a nice stopover and we didn't see any Migs or missiles, a good thing.

With the weather good we flew and flew a lot, moving as much freight as possible. Daylight in the summer months lasted about twenty-hours in Bethel. Burn out can be a concern. Measuring time by daylight is unusual; my body says go, but my brain says no. Everybody deals with it differently. As pilots we were governed by the Federal Aviation Regulations (FAR) of twelve hours of duty time and ten hours of flight time in a twenty-four hour period. This northern phenomena is felt in states like Michigan, however nowhere to this degree. And the reverse, very little daylight in the winter months is a nightmare.

Poor weather is another side of flying hard and working long hours in good weather. No flying means nothing to do. This happens quite frequently, sometimes for a day and sometimes for three or four. Entertainment is virtually nonexistent in the bush. Personal motivation is needed to read a good book, listen to short wave radio, explore the outdoors, write letters home or cook. To make the no-fly days tolerable. Another distraction from boredom was alcohol. Pilots enjoy drinking and drinking together while swapping stories, laughing, telling jokes and building their egos. When drinking, we didn't leave the apartment. "There are strange things done in the midnight sun." This is a passage from a poem "The Cremation of Sam Magee" by Robert W. Service, a wonderful poem of the Alaska past.

As my tour in Bethel was coming to an end thoughts of my family and my real home became pleasant thoughts. Although the thought of switching from bush life to life in the real world was tough. After three weeks of living outside the world of the lower forty-eight states I became comfortable with the way of life and my job. Even with all the huge changes in my conditions, and feelings of loneliness and great distance from my loved ones, this life fit me. Bush life became alluring. I found a purpose to life, a calling, and even with all the chaos and calamity involved with daily life in the bush, I loved it. The day finally came for me to say goodbye to Bethel and begin my journey to Michigan leaving behind the flying, the sights, sounds, smells, and faces of the bush. I had become part of their world.

My trip started on board a weeney bird B-737 combi to Anchorage, with a layover of almost ten hours. I secured a room at the hotel, trying to start my acclimation back to the world. After some sleep, and then an Alaskan king crab dinner at Elevation 92, the best seafood restaurant in Anchorage. I felt better. The next leg of this trip will take me from Anchorage to Seattle (SeaTac airport) then on to Chicago (O'Hare) and finally, Detroit Metro.

My departure time was midnight (a true red eye), on Northwest Airlines B-727. The atmosphere on this flight reminded me of a sleeper car on a train with lights very low in the cabin and little movement. Even the cabin crew caught some shut-eye, but I was wide awake. The thought of seeing my wife and family kept my mind swirling.

After a two-hour layover in Seattle, I boarded a DC-10 for Chicago. It was May 18, 1980. Our first route took us just north of Mt. St. Helen on a sunny clear day I observed the mountain from my tiny window. It had been rumbling and blowing smoke for the past few months, but on this fly-over view it was quiet. But about fifteen minutes later the captain came on the intercom to inform us that Mt. St. Helen just blew its top and there was smoke and ash going to fifty thousand feet. To be able to view this from our altitude of thirty eight thousand feet would have been specular, however the captain chose to press on. The strangest part of this trip for me came just after the captain's announcement. Two passengers began to walk the aisles, looking very closely at all the seats. The other odd thing was there clothing. One in blue shirt and gray coat, the other in gray shirt and blue coat. I don't know to this day if I was lost in transition or hallucinating, but these guys were looking for something, maybe a vision into the future.

I spent the weekend acclimating from jet lag and culture shock, and reuniting with my family. Mt. St. Helen showed itself over Detroit a couple of days later. Ash could be seen in the higher altitudes over the area, just a footprint of the size of that explosion.

The hardest part of my dual jobs was coming back to the office. The company expected me to be on the job, in the office, Monday morning. Coming from such a different environment, compared to where I was now created a deep conflict in my mind, but ultimately working itself out with patience and inner strength.

During my travels home I gave a lot of thought to my future and how I could make things easier for all of the family. The one thing that would make it very workable for me would be to move the family, Connie and Laura to Anchorage. Connie knew what my job meant to me in Alaska. She was always a trooper and open to new experiences. So when I proposed the idea to her she agreed somewhat, not ruling it out completely, and for me, that was a victory. I explained to her that Anchorage is like any town USA, with all the stores she could want, and weather very similar to Michigan. My wheels were turning. We may be able to put this deal together yet.

When the time approached for me to rotate back to Bethel, I became energized. The thought of flying in the bush again and operating on the edge, instilled life into me. My focus became razor-sharp. I was where I wanted to be. I had reached a point of fulfillment in a lifelong dream. This was a natural high.

The most difficult time came when saying goodbye to Connie and Laura. With this departure I carried the flicker in my heart that we may be changing these goodbyes for a much closer arrangement. Boarding the airliner to take me back, I focused on the job at hand, the sadness of leaving disappeared quickly. My upbeat personality emerged. This trip consisted of a stop in Chicago, one plane change, to a B-747 then direct to Anchorage. This is about as good as it can get.

Landing at Anchorage I was able to catch the Weeney bird to Bethel later that day. Getting reacquainted with the guys felt good; nothing really changed although some bad weather set in which halted the flying for a time.

I was back in the saddle as the flying resumed. Servicing the local villages with packages of all types and relearning my bush flying techniques felt good. Life back in Bethel returned to normal, as normal as Bethel can be.

Then the bombshell hit on my last week in town. Rod Thompson flew out with the news. The company lost contract bids for the Skyvan, and operations would end soon. I was shocked! How can a solid set-up end so fast? Alaska became Skyhawk's life boat. Where can it go from here? The feeling of being stranded on a small island in a big ocean consumed my thoughts. After finishing the week's flying, I headed for Michigan. The company knew of our problem and a solution must be found.

These contracts that were let out for bid by companies needing air service were all business. Wherever they could save money they did. That was part of the reason the contracts were short in duration and air charter companies were willing to do almost anything to secure a flying contract not a comfortable position for even the most established air charter companies.

At the office in Dearborn discussions began with the president and CFO on the future of Skyhawk Air Services and the Skyvan. The Alaskan possibilities were being covered by Rod Thompson and I began taking out ads in the trade publications, hoping for anything. The conversation changed to selling the Skyvan, an option that made me cringe. The $9,800-a-month payment would be a huge drain without revenue. Things must happen fast to save the operation.

A couple of weeks passed with no change. Rod, in Anchorage got an inquiry about purchasing the Skyvan through Cape Smythe Air Service located in Barrow, Alaska, and an established operator in the region. Skyhawk Air Services was ready to make a move. Our CFO and I traveled to Barrow. Bush Air would move 50DA from Bethel to Barrow. After a price was agreed to, the training and FAA certification became the final concern. Jim Scott from Summit Airlines conducted initial training on the Skyvan. 50DA was flown to Fairbanks for FAA inspection, a trip I declined though a bad choice on my part. My emotions got the best of me and I felt an obligation to stay with my boss in Barrow. With all the details completed, and cash wired to the bank, we departed Barrow. That was the last time I saw 50DA and Alaska.

Bethel radar antenna

rear door open construction load

tundra view

offloading fuel load

Chapter Forty

Probing for a Job Again

Nothing is so painful to the human mind as a great and sudden change.

—Mary Shelley

Back home the parent company retained me on the payroll to dissolve Skyhawk and tie up loose ends. My dream that came true was gone. Once again I'm weighted down. During these times life is so difficult. How do I pick up the pieces? Where do I turn? All my mental strength and desire is lost, vanished. I've failed again. My only desire is to conceal this thought from my loved ones. This will remain my secret.

The obvious tasks were put into action: filing for unemployment benefits, rewriting my resume, and sending a message to all that may be helpful in my predicament to find employment. This was a difficult undertaking. In my mind, this was just short of begging, and feeling worthless. I continued going through the motions. With all my lines in the water, there wasn't much biting.

Making contact with an old flying friend, Jeff Kilponen, my spirit lifted. He informed me of a possible job with the company he worked for, Interstate Airlines based at Willow Run Airport. He flew as captain on their Convair 580 Turboprop freighter. I felt uplifted, with the possibility of some life in a dismal picture. The one catch, ground school on the 580 must be completed before hiring.

Finding somewhere to attend ground school led me back to Summit Airlines. When Summit upgraded from the Skyvan, to the 580 as their new freight hauler, they began running ground school classes on a regular basis. I made contact with their training department and obtained the class schedule. It would cost one thousand dollars with room and board extra. Money was an issue and a huge hurdle. Honestly, I don't know how Connie and I pulled it off, but we did. I also received another savings. Summit Airlines allowed me jump seat authorization on one of their flights out of Metro to Phillie, a big cost savings.

On October 14, 1981, I left for Philadelphia. As luck would have it we were delayed leaving DTW by a mechanical problem. Finally airborne, our route took us through JFK then on to PHI, arriving four hours late to class. Understanding of my situation and being on a Summit flight, they made adjustments and fit me in.

The class of three instructors all took turns in their field of expertise with six students. The class went great; good instruction and lots of information. I learned the 580 is a very complex aircraft I also learned that Summit needed F/Os (first officers). After three days of class we all received certificates of completion. I searched for a ride back to Detroit, spotting a trip to DTW on the scheduling board for 10:00 p.m. They had my name on the jump seat. Flying back the crew were pleasant and inquisitive. Over Lake Erie I was asked to fly the approach into Metro. I took the controls of the 580 over the lake. In the darkness we entered the Detroit Metropolitan area. With all the lights and coming from an unfamiliar direction, in a complex airplane I had never flown I did a poorly. And I knew it. Later I realized that this flight was my final exam with Summit Airlines to determine if they had interest in hiring me. I never heard from Summit.

The main reason for 580 ground school was employment with Interstate Airlines. But this also fell through with lots of false promises.

Chapter Forty-One

Losing Control and Lost Dignity

We do not see things as they are. We see things as we are.

—Dad

Feelings of failure filled my mind. As hard as I worked to overcome them, they controlled me. Retracing all my past successes and searching for positive ideas did not help me at all, but only transformed into delusions and fake images. This state of mind only grew with time, driving me into a reclusive state of behavior.

One day my mother called to inform me that Mrs. Malcolm a family friend from the old neighborhood had passed. She asked if I would go the funeral home with her. I said yes. Mom offered to pick me up at seven o'clock. When she arrived, I lost it. In tears I told her I couldn't go, I was a mess. Only as mothers can do, she gave me a hug and said it's all okay and then left. My next action was extremely bazaar. I went out to our Subaru wagon, opened the lift gate and climbed inside. I positioned myself in a fetal position while shaking and crying. Connie came out to find me in this condition.

My challenge became concealing my behavior from my wife and daughter. This was my secret, and I was determined to conceal it from them. During my secret life I was up early making coffee, and lunches, doing anything I could to get their day off to a normal start. As they prepared for the day I created activities making busy work and small talk, rather than show any signs of my true inner feelings. Once I sent them on their way, my day alone in the house began. Trying to contain my depressed feelings I listened to music, but found it too interrupting. I tried reading, but could not focus, then television, my mind only wandered. Finally, I just sat in a chair and attempted to think myself out of this critical depression. Finding no relief, the helpless terrifying ideas began to clog my brain.

The afternoon brought Laura home first and my disguise went up. She would usually ask to go to a friend's house to hang out until dinner. Then Connie's arrival and more small talk until dinner. This routine continued until one day Connie returned from work saying that she had been in contact with a doctor, a psychiatrist and thought it would be good for me to make an appointment. I responded extremely negatively to her. Seeing one would ruin my aviation career. This was out of the question. The idea vanished.

Time pressed on and my depression deepened, I began to spend more time in the basement staring at the walls. Thoughts of despair and hopelessness consumed me, leading to suicidal thoughts as the only way to end this pain. I pondered this belief for some time while positioning my loaded .38-caliber pistol near my seat in the basement.

Two things protected me from this horrid thought I planned to undertake. One was my wife and daughter. I could not put them through the sight that I would leave them with, and the shame. The other and equally strong conviction was my faith in Jesus Christ. I knew that suicide was a sin. Only He knows the time we are to leave this earth, not me. He died for me, to save me. When Connie returned from work that day I asked her to make an appointment for me to see the psychiatrist. I was ready.

Dr. Jamie Ajala became the first in a long list of psychiatrists I retained. His evaluation was quick and to the point. Noting I was severely depressed and suicidal he recommended immediate hospitalization. I realized my thoughts and feelings were wrong. Scared and extremely confused, the plans were made for my hospital admission to Oakwood Hospital in Dearborn, Michigan.

During the admission process Connie answered most of the questions. I sat in a trance. After all the formalities were completed we were escorted to the psychiatric ward, the top floor, the "penthouse" as it is called by the residents. A common practice in multi-level hospitals is to designate the top floor for psychiatric care.

Entering the ward a nurse and aide showed me my room, and then took us on a short tour of the floor. My mind raced, observing all the puzzling people. I'm terrified. Fear of the unknown and visions from all the movies about the nut house chilled my thoughts. The time came to say goodbye to Connie, my last touch with a normal life. My final request to her was not to allow visitors to see me. I felt so ashamed of my situation. I could not bear to see anyone, my daughter, my parents, other family or friends, no one but her. Connie promised to honor my request. I just could not handle that burden. I had enough other baggage to carry. My thoughts were consumed by this indignity-being the lowest of the lowest form of human existence. Saying our goodbyes, I felt the relief she showed, leaving me here, and knowing I would be safe and protected. She promised to return.

Even as depressed as I was, and my thought process almost paralyzed I wanted to explore the layout of my new environment. I entered the open space. People were sitting in this area talking, reading and just sitting. Some looked very distant. Off to one side was a Ping-Pong table. I sensed staff was always around, trying to be inconspicuous but always observing and being sociable. This was the norm.

My small bag containing personal things was checked and returned. The staff, notified by my doctor of his sincere concern and potential risk of suicide, ordered suicide watch for me. This action, a rather severe procedure, consisted of constant surveillance by a staff member 24-7. I was never left alone. Eating, sleeping, showering, reading, talking, using the restroom, I was observed. At meals my normal eating utensils were replaced with plastic silverware, plates and cups, a humiliating experience.

As always I tried to make the most of my situation by adapting. This chaos will not control me; I still could move about in my world freely, yet knowing I was constantly scrutinized. In less than three days I proved that I would not harm myself. The suicide watch was lifted. Emotionally this action was grueling and thankfully it ended.

Life became predictable, boring and dull. But mingling with the other patients, I became comfortable with them. I discovered how "normal" they were. I enjoyed conversations and appreciated how similar our lives were. Some preferred no communication.

To fill the daily void the staff conducted classes consisting of occupational therapy. The group sessions were different. Open discussions were held with patients talking about depression, family life, alcoholism, drug addiction, self-esteem, and jobs. My thoughts became more solid and realistic about drugs and alcohol. How and why they were choices I made in my life. Not as an addiction but self-medicating my pain. Listening to other people in group describe their manic phases humbled me to realize my thinking was not as genius as I believed it was. Group sessions helped to give insight to my issues from a different realistic personal view. The feelings were genuine. Group also helped occupy time, and sometimes even became intense.

In my most lonely times, lying in bed late at night with tears in my eyes, I reflected on where I am and how I got to this point of my life. This unhinged my thinking. Is this my future? Will I be this way forever? Is this just a bump in the road and then everything will go back to normal? Little did I know then, that this reflection would haunt and confuse my mind for many years to come.

Another introduction to my life in the psych ward exposed me to psychotropic drugs. I learned their use was horrific, medicine's answer to everything. Drugs, with so many strange and multiple names and dosages of all proportions astounded me. The pills were dispensed out of a small locked room. At the appointed time all patients received their medications in a small container after being identified by their wristband. Then we were offered fruit juice or water to swallow the drugs, in front of a nurse. This ritual was performed four times a day. The "cattle call" routine created a zombie like mood. This routine was my first exposure to prescribed drugs. My main issue at the time was depression. At first I showed no signs of relief, the drugs just clouded my mind and thoughts. The "grab bag" approach in adjusting medication began.

During one of these periods a strong craving overcame me, I wanted chocolate. I went to the nurse's station and asked for a pass to visit the lobby. This was granted to patients who the staff felt trustworthy. Receiving approval I headed to the elevator. At the ground floor I hurried into the gift shop and grabbed the biggest candy bar I could find, made payment and proceeded to the lobby. After devouring the extra-large bar my craving persisted and I returned to the gift shop to buy another. This helped my craving somewhat. Returning to the unit I still questioned this behavior. Never being a chocoholic, I learned this issue emerged as a side effect to of one of my anti-depressants.

Surprisingly, another effect from this drug helped my depression. As low as I had plunged, the bad thoughts were being lifted. As hard as I tried to convince myself that I'm down and depressed, this uplifting mood overruled. I tried hard to continue my depressed feelings to no avail; my depressed thoughts lifted, the first sign that drugs do work.

Sessions with my doctor occurred two to three times a week, depending on his schedule and rounds. We mostly discussed my basic well-being and how I planned to deal with life events after going home, no ground breaking concepts just thoughts. During my hospital time my attitude improved, but I hadn't found my inner self. I was still lost and gained little comfort.

One of the patients in the ward really stood out. He was a big man with the looks of a "biker" type. At times when calm and collected he socialized with other patients. However, this day a heated discussion began. As his anger intensified he captured everyone's attention on the floor. He became physical, pounding and jumping around definitely out of control. All of a sudden he jumped high, and with both fists smashed a large clock on the wall above the nurse's station. The sound of the impact and the glass shattering created chaos. Aides quickly subdued him. His hands were bloody, making the counter at the nurse's station resemble a crime scene. Quickly they moved him to the ER where doctors mended his hands. The cleaning staff cleaned the mess and returned the area to normal. The show of uncontrolled anger shocked us all. It was a sign of just how dangerous a psychiatric hospital can be, even though the staff worked at downplaying the incident.

After twenty-three days in the penthouse at Oakwood my doctor and staff concluded I was well enough to join the world and go home. I missed my family and home but felt unsure about how well I was. With my discharge orders my small bag of personal belongings and a bag of pills, Connie chauffeured me home. After completing my first psychiatric hospital stay it felt surreal as I walked into our little duplex.

I needed to decompress. Laura was not home from school yet. Connie and I sat in our living room and made small talk. Having thoughts of being here before my hospitalization, and knowing that I was still sick, I wondered if I could handle it. Later that day I reunited with Laura. This was a sincere worry for me. What would she think of me (now that the cat is out of the bag)? With a new title, "crazy."

I was still searching to win her acceptance in my new role as dad since I had adopted Laura just two years ago. To my amazement our reuniting went fine. She talked about school and her friends in a very relaxed manner. She then asked permission to go play at her friend's house. A burden had been lifted from my confused mind. I embraced both relief and a little peace.

My home life returned to a normal atmosphere and shortly into a routine. Connie was off to work, Laura back in school and me at home alone. The fears and the walls were back, "What is wrong with me?" I must come out of this trap. "I can do it." The guy who has done so much can do it. But the wicked thoughts overwhelmed me. I'm hopeless, condemned to this living hell. I'm a recluse fearful of everything. My life to this point was not real. This is my reality.

When Connie returned from work one day she knew things were unmanageable again. Instead of waiting for my next appointment she called Dr. Ajala and I saw him the next morning. His assessment came quickly. I was admitted again to Oakwood. As hard as I resisted re-entering the psychiatric hospital, I retraced my steps with no resistance.

The mission of this trip would be an attempt to counter suicidal thoughts and break down the walls of fear and inward captivity. Entering the unit was less of a fear this time. I entered this world as an old hand now. Some patients were still there from my previous visit, and they filled me in on recent stories. New to this visit was Ping-Pong, a game I played and enjoyed. Patients took turns and a competition grew while we got our exercise and passed the time.

Later in the week a new patient arrived; a little quiet mailman who lived in the area. He seemed normal, and friendly. No one knew his reason for being admitted. For the next few days the mailman and I played Ping-Pong, beating me more than a few times. He seemed to enjoy the games.

One morning I heard a commotion coming from the room next to me. Then shouts for help. Worried, I ran out of my room and into the next. The mailman was suspended from the floor hanging lifeless with one end of his belt wrapped around his neck, the other strapped to the top of the closet door. Completely motionless, his head leaned forward, lifeless. I froze, unable to move. Looking at him, I knew he was gone, Realizing there was a call for help I made no effort to move. Like a statue I stood envisioning the lifeless body.

Quickly people entered the room, desperately working to release his listless body onto the floor. Things were hectic. I left the room. Entering the hall, I heard the call, "Code blue, fifth floor." In shock I re-entered my room, thinking of our Ping-Pong game just the night before. Now he's gone. How can that be? Why wasn't he on suicide watch? Hurriedly his body was transported to the ER. Then the official word came, the mailman was dead. The atmosphere on the floor became surreal. The staff, in shock, tried to downplay the episode, to maintain calm and normalcy. Although thoughts of the mailman were swirling in my brain the need to focus on my goals and therapy still were in play.

My therapy involved getting back into society and learning to function again. The plan included having my car in the parking lot for use when authorized. The day of the suicide I was to drive home and visit with my family. The nurses were extremely hesitant to release my keys. I waited, returning in an hour with the same request. The concern was whether this issue would affect my judgment and be a problem. I assured them I would be fine. Not seeing my family would be a greater issue. With profound reluctance I received my keys.

I was enjoying my visit home. During conversation I informed Connie I was still shocked by the hospital incident. Yet we ended the day with a wonderful meal prepared by my wife, said our goodbyes, and I drove myself back to Oakwood.

Back at the penthouse, things changed a bit. The reality of the mailman gone from our group still disturbed fellow patients. And staff hid their grief so as not to upset us. The thought of a suicide in a psychiatric hospital must have shaken them to their souls. Death is so real. I wanted to get well and not end up like the mailman. His instant on earth had ended.

The loss of the mailman by suicide affected me in many ways. It left me with so many questions and painful feelings. After many years of trials and tribulations I concluded that God put me in that room that morning of the hanging, to have me witness the reality of taking one's life; to see it first hand, in all the detail, and how real death is. I truly believe God took one soul to save another. I can honestly reveal that since my exposure to those images, no suicidal thoughts have entered my mind. A life lost saved another.

With the help of the right medication and my inner desire for progress, things were getting clearer even after this traumatic incident. My days were brighter with a more optimistic outlook and showed signs of my previous personality.

Although it was a psychiatric ward, one way that helped me and other patents were the volunteers they made days more enjoyable. A very kind hospital volunteer visited us who reminded me of a mix between Santa Claus and Captain Kangaroo. Everyone enjoyed seeing him on the ward whether he was teaching us to make balloon figures or just visiting with us. Everyone was able to feel his presence and affection. The memory of this gentleman's open, loving, caring, and selfless personality provided a gleam of hope in this very dark time of my life. The feelings he created within me will remain forever.

Even as slow as time moved, it did march on. It wasn't long before talk began about my departure. I did feel I had a better grip on my life and depression. Fear of the outside world disappeared from my thoughts. Medications and my experience in the psychiatric floor were working. Although I was still moving slow and not acting like my old self, I really wanted a new chance to be in control of my actions and re-adjust to a normal life. I still felt trapped in my world with thoughts like "I can't." I searched for my past motivation, determination, and get up and go, but this attitude wasn't there yet.

Time marched on. I knew flying was out of the question, psychiatric meds took care of that. My thoughts of working in an office with lots of people did not excite me. I never imagined being in a people person job, although my life has been surrounded by people. But not now.

Connie and I had been trying to get pregnant for some time with no success. With my diagnosis of manic depression and informed that it is a hereditary illness, our desire for children ended. Having my adopted daughter, Laura, helped me, but the thought of never fathering a child weighted heavily on me. It saddens me to this day. Consulting my psychiatrist I learned the chances of children developing manic depressive illness are no different than any other of the inherited illnesses. We were scared and uneducated, and the ache remains.

Mental illness carries such heavy baggage. Aside from my diagnosis, society creates obstacles that cast aside the mentally ill. Thoughts expressed like, "I never want to be like that," and "It's best to stay as far away from them as you can," and "Act like they don't exist, then maybe they will go away." This is the struggle of the mentally ill and my struggle. It's often more debilitating than the diagnosis. This war is a lonely, isolated, shameful battle.

Depression became less of a concern in my activities. The other demon mania, was now entering my life. As part of the manic-depression diagnosis. Becoming less of a lifeless, imprisoned, suicidal being, I was then into a busy, get it done, must-happen-now mode. Leaving the chains of depression one would think the storm had passed, but not so. Mania is just as threatening as or more so than depression. Mania always leads to out-of-control behavior, crumbing families, financial disaster and deadly places. Anyone looking to find peace with manic depressive illness in its untreated state will find no relief, only human tragedy. If mania could be bottled and distributed in controlled doses, human productivity would increase to record levels.

Chapter Forty-Two

Finding Menial Work and Crisis

God gives the nuts, but he does not crack them.
—Old Proverb

After being discharged from Oakwood I needed to start living a different life style from my past days. I desperately needed to replenish our cash flow. Being offered a job cutting lawns with a neighbor, Mr. Lee. He operated his own service in the area and had developed a good-sized clientele. I accepted his offer and began pushing a Lawn Boy lawnmower for five dollars per hour, cash. Although a far cry from my previous salary, I was grateful to be working, creating action and income, making a step forward. Work continued fairly steadily and my home life improved. Mr. Lee and I drove his old van with trailer from house to house cutting lawns and any other small jobs customers requested. He was a very kind, soft-spoken, hardworking man, a Southerner with an accent and little formal education. I hope he recognized what an important part he played in my recovery. During my time with Mr. Lee, pushing the lawnmower instilled confidence and a yearning to do more. Mr. Lee received requests to do some garage and house painting from customers. Not wanting to upset any customers, we took the first one on. I soon realized Mr. Lee's distaste for painting, and it became obvious this was not his forte. With that thought he offered me all the painting requests, which I enthusiastically agreed to.

My focus went from lawn cutting to exterior painting. My first job was a garage for an elderly widowed lady which helped build my confidence and self-esteem. My progress was slow and tedious but I wanted and needed perfect results. Upon completion I delivered a great finished product and was rewarded with a nice tip.

One job seemed to lead to another and getting the work finished became a big issue. Thinking of how to increase production, spraying in place of brushing came to mind. Quickly I assembled equipment for the task. With my new equipment the work began. Soon I learned how to deal with new issues; preparation time, covering non-painted areas, overspray, and paint quality. After overcoming these issues, I completed several jobs. The bottom line profit was still weak, as well as my enthusiasm.

At home I retreated to my basement workshop making plans with my mind in over-drive. I stayed up nights planning mostly nothing. A friend of mine, Tim Cook, was building a true log cabin by hand up north and asked if I would come and help him out. I loved the outdoors and jumped at the chance.

We took a long weekend and worked on the cabin building the walls. Along with Tim's brother, Steve, we made good progress. On the property Tim parked a small travel trailer to use as a base camp for the project. We cooked, slept and entertained ourselves in it. The entertainment consisted of drinking and smoking pot (my favorite), not so much the alcohol. We all had fun while making progress on the cabin.

Returning home with no painting to do, I occupied my time doing nothing, but stayed busy smoking pot. I was convinced this would not hurt my condition and probably help. After some time Connie was getting wise to my self-medication and some heated arguments erupted. One night I had my fill and made the decision to pack all my gear, including guns and head to Tim's cabin. I made sure not to reveal my destination. With the Subaru loaded I departed.

Having the best of intensions, I knew for sure I was doing the correct thing. Arriving late at the cabin in the woods, alone, my thoughts raced about all the things I would accomplish at the cabin. But then those thoughts faded. Alone in the dark woods my plan changed. I decided to find a comfortable place to spend the night and regroup.

Back in the Subaru I headed to Traverse City, Michigan. The drive took over an hour. My thoughts still in overdrive, I arrived in the city and decided on the Holiday Inn because it was near the water. Checking in, I handed the receptionist my American Express Card (not that my lifestyle warranted one—it was a leftover from my flying days). Grabbing my gear from the car including my guns I went up to my room. I arranged my room to my liking and attempted to get some sleep. Manic and functioning in high gear, sleep did not work. I passed time by walking the halls of the hotel. All night I roamed. Only the security people were around. Otherwise the motel was empty. My roaming created interesting activity for security that night.

With the sun up and the day beginning, my stomach reminded me it needed some attention. Walking through the lobby I spotted a door that looked like an entry to the restaurant. Long windows exposed a beautiful view of Grand Traverse Bay. I walked in and picked a booth by the windows I saw no one.

Viewing the water and a large boat motoring out into Lake Michigan created a tranquil and peaceful image for me. A waitress entered from the other side. In a very calm voice I ordered a beer. In a somewhat alarmed voice, she said, "We're not open and you have to leave." Trying to retain my tranquil thoughts, I responded to her, "When you open, I'll have a beer." Walking toward me, she responded, "No, you have to leave now." I conveyed my desire to just sit and not bother anyone. (There was no one to bother.) I did not plan to leave, but she replied, "Oh, yes, you will."

The manager arrived at my booth, reiterating that I had to leave. I tried to explain my position. I entered as a guest of the hotel, sat at a seat making no demands and planned to stay seated. But he was telling me I must leave. He replied, "Yes." At this point with my position firm, I responded, "I'm not leaving." With a look of determination, he departed.

Within minutes I spotted two uniformed police officers approaching my booth. With very few words spoken they grabbed me from behind and ripped me out of the booth. This action automatically threw me into a defensive mode. On the floor I began to defend myself from their attack. I am delighted to say that I kept the two cops busy for a fair amount of time. Finally, I succumbed to their force. They won. Handcuffs were applied to my wrists behind my back. I was trained in the Air Force police school and had witnessed this type of conduct before. It was not new to me.

All the way to the station from the back seat of their patrol car I taunted them. I complimented them on their technique on arresting a non-violent, unarmed person. I goaded them, saying it takes a lot of courage to double team a non-aggressive, unarmed man. This became my only gratification after my arrest.

The booking process was very vague, probably due to the trauma of my arrest. After the formalities in the booking room, I was escorted to a cell. My small confined world shocked me as it opened to reveal a metal commode/sink combo, a single metal bed bolted to the floor and a very thin mattress. My mind began racing. This is not normal. I belonged on the outside not the inside. I was going nowhere. Trying to organize a plan for my immediate future became difficult, especially considering I had no sleep or medication for two days deepening my madness. Fear and mania kept me in high gear,

I am totally alone and no one knows where I am but the cops. Isolated from my loved ones, I felt like I could have been on the Moon. If anything is going to happen I must initiate it. My only tool was my voice. Through the little cell window of the steel door, I yelled, "I need my meds! I need food! Let me out of here!" Multiple times my requests were ignored. Numerus times the jailer peered into my cell. His surveillance became very annoying. I asked him to stop, but he didn't. So I worked out a fix for the problem. Moving the mattress from my bunk into the door-way blocked his view. No longer being observed like a caged animal in a zoo, I patted myself on the back and had a good chuckle. My victory was short lived. Soon after, my cell door opened and an arm grabbed my mattress and pulled it out, never to be seen again. I think this lesson fell under the category, good idea bad results.

My arrest took place on a Friday morning. I would be in jail at least until Monday when I would appear in court. I could not comprehend spending time in such a small area in these conditions. Influenced by the injustice cast upon me, as I saw made me determined to fight on. The first days I refused any food.

Then I made the discovery that I had a neighbor. He began talking and asking questions in a somewhat calm and normal voice. I never saw his face. It helped to bring me back to some form of reality and grounded me. During our conversations I could tell this was not his first visit to jail. By the fourth day my mind and body were broken. The latest news was that I wasn't going to court, but being transferred to the Traverse City Regional Psychiatric Hospital.

Chapter Forty-Three

The Feared State Mental Sanatorium

Fear not tomorrow. God is already there.
—E. C. Mckenzie, *Quips and Quotes*

On Tuesday in Traverse City my wife received a call informing her of my whereabouts. She had no idea of my location since I left Thursday evening. She was informed by the prosecuting attorney that he wanted to meet with her.

During the meeting he explained the charges against me and some of the reasons that landed me in jail, wandering the floors throughout the night and having guns in my room. And of course, the restaurant ordeal. Charges would be dropped if I would voluntarily sign myself into the state hospital. The attorney and Connie's big concern was that by law I could sign myself out within seventy two hours.

Arriving at the jail Connie saw me for the first time in five days. In that time I rested very little and had not taken a shower or shaved. The guard shuffled me into the room in shackles wearing an orange jumpsuit. The proposal was explained to me. Definitely not wanting to remain in jail, but scared to death about the state hospital, I made my choice. Ignoring my fears I signed the papers to enter the hospital. Everyone showed concern about signing myself out in three days. I assured them that was not my intention.

My mind and body confused like nothing I had experienced before. I was so ashamed for my wife to see me in this state. Connie and I said our goodbyes. Her strength through this was incredible. Few people could endure this hardship and stress the way she did.

Based on the information given to the hospital from the police, the staff proceeded very cautiously. The customary procedure in psychiatric hospitals is to administer Thorazine, a powerful anti-psychotic. All I wanted was peace and sleep, which did happen.

After a long sleep and still under the effects of the Thorazine, I got my first shower and shave in six days. Even being drugged things greatly improved. The staff appeared friendly and helpful.

Escorted to the cafeteria and envisioning the worst of the worst in hospital food, I was blown away by the food line. Everything looked fresh and smelled delicious. It was just like home-cooked food prepared with great care, the little old ladies gave me the impression of being just like Grandmas. I enjoyed the food so much, recognizing another little touch with reality, a welcome feeling to my world. I wondered if this was a special meal or if all the meals were this good. Food is an amazing equalizer and a peaceful act.

Everything seemed huge, with tall ceilings, and walls with big doors. My room, with a single steel bed and an old chair and dresser, created an impersonal feeling. Only having the clothes given me in exchange for the orange jump suit, I needed clothes. A staff member escorted me into a room that contained tons of clothes, not new, but nice. I grabbed pajamas, a robe, slippers, t-shirts and pants. This really uplifted my spirits. My fears and nightmares of the state hospital began to fade.

My first full day started early with breakfast, another great meal, then moved to the day room. This room held fifty patients (its size could hold a hundred and fifty) with different types of chairs, couches, tables, a TV and Ping-Pong table. Many patients seemed normal, some withdrawn and some just plain out of it. The biggest surprise for me was comparing this to the Oakwood Hospital (my only comparisons.) Their staff was ample and always felt nearby.

Here I had to seek out staff. Their responsibility encompassed fifty patients, with two nurses and three attendants on the day shift, less on the other shifts. The doctors moved in and out throughout the day.

I planned to mingle and strike up conversations with people that seemed approachable. It's interesting as time passes the things learned. My outgoing personality helped. Some of my hospital friends, Mike, Francis, Janine. We enjoyed each other's company. Always present was the undercurrent that we were sick and in this hospital for a reason.

As days passed, my desire increased to understand my unending difficulties and find the answer to the big question, "How do I keep from ending up in these places?" I became close to Nurse Ruth. She was one of the nicest people I have ever known in my life. She carried a heavy personal burden but concealed it well. She always maintained a calm and grace about her. In one of our conversations she shared with me some of her personal pain. Her son was killed in the Vietnam War. Ruth always displayed passion in her job. Motivated to push on through difficult situations, I believed helped her to deal with her own loss. One day I approached Ruth with a question. Could she find books, magazines, any articles on manic depression for me? I wanted all the information I could on this illness. I want to beat it, somehow. A few days later she handed me a book that she explained should be helpful in my study of my mental illness. I started to read *A Mind That Found Itself* by Clifford Whittingham Beers (copyright 1908, reprinted forty-one times since first publication). My thoughts were confused. I thought that Ruth would bring me medical information discussing all the studies and testing done recently, not a book from the turn of the century. I was puzzled. It took me some time to grasp the direction she was taking me. The book relates the story of a man who graduated from Yale and had been troubled mentally and emotionally for a long time. His solution for his problem was suicide. He jumped out of an upper floor window of his parents' home. Unsuccessful in his attempt, he spent many months recovering physically and emotionally. From his experience he went on to become one of the most vocal advocates for the mentally ill in America for reform and humane treatment. He established the American Foundation for Mental Hygiene, Inc. and operated it until his death in 1943.

I now understand Ruth's point and direction with this book. The author survived mental illness and went on to do great things by himself, with only his desire and a little money. His message and Ruth's was that anyone of us have the capability to do the same. Our individual message is just a part of the picture. Reaching out to others on the edge or beyond is what matters. Her ability to inject personal, unparalleled experiences that she survived and to help others become competent to live with our normal lives was Ruth's goal. (Idea-plan). It took years of therapy, personal evaluation, setbacks, honesty, and faith in God for me to truly understand Ruth's rationale for selecting this book for me. It continues to help me understand my illness.

My routine in this state hospital continued. Cutting back on the powerful drugs, I was able to identify with some patients. The good food made this place nicer than I ever thought possible. I experienced some difficulty as I continued reading my book, A *Mind That Found Itself.* The language took on different pulses and used words that are not familiar to readers today. One of my favorite words from the book was "phantasmagoric," meaning a fantastic sequence of haphazardly associated imagery, as seen in dreams or fever. I believe that I can associate some of my behavior this way. Another word that I liked was "philanthropy," a desire to help mankind as shown by gifts to charitable or humanitarian institutions; benevolence. A goal I hope to work on before I depart this world.

Even as I attempted to improve my life, bizarre events were not far away. Sounds from inside the walls became most shocking. From my C-3 corner I would hear the most awful horrible human screams of emotional pain, and sounds of dying. This could be heard mainly at night and made me very sad. I know what it feels and looks like to be out of my mind now I know what it sounds like as well.

The weekends, as in any hospital, are less hectic with less staff and a slower pace. On this particular Sunday, my first one in the hospital, something unusual took place. I realized that I wasn't able to urinate. The first few times unsuccessful at the urinal did not worry me. By the afternoon with still no relief I searched for a doctor. There was only one on duty I asked to talk with her when she returned. Finally, I met with the staff doctor. I began to communicate to her my situation. Then in a hurried way, she told me to do all the things that I have already done. She continued to tell me to keep doing the things I've already done as she departs for the day. Things are getting worse. My stomach is getting hard and I'm feeling more uncomfortable. The shift change was made. Midnight Baldy and Art came on duty. Finally, in desperation, I talked with Midnight Baldy, and he performed a brief exam. He relayed to Art that my stomach was distended, and I needed to be catheterized now. This is one of my first times to hear that word, and even with all the bad allegations, I welcomed it. The scene was far from a hospital setting. I was lying on my bed and Art left to get the roller-mop bucket to collect my urine. Baldy, having the most experience in this (a retired chief from the Coast Guard) but still only an aide, prepared the kit. At this point I had no relief and hurt severely, Baldy knew the consequences if there wasn't urine flowing soon. I don't know if Baldy was good or lucky. I was in so much pain the only thing I felt was the flow of urine. As the bag filled, Art transferred the contents into the mop bucket. In the end everything worked out and I literally never felt so relieved in my life. Leave it to the people with the least medical experience and the most common sense to get the job done. I was grateful to Art and Midnight Baldy. Never did I acquire a medical reason for this problem, but I'm sure it was related to medications.

Feeling like the Lone Ranger, with no one for support and completely alone and on my own, drained my thinking. After Connie's return home from her visit with the prosecuting attorney, things began to happen. Plans to pick up my car (impounded by the cops) were made. Connie and my brother Tom flew up on North Central Airlines to Traverse City and retrieved my personal belongings from the Holiday Inn (everything but my guns) and the car from the police pound.

On their way out of town they stopped to see me. I was still in pretty bad shape. Connie informed me of a planned family meeting the next day to discuss getting me home. It all sounded good but all

I wanted to do was hug and hold Connie, I so missed the closeness of family life. In a short time the visit ended. I felt good knowing my family would help me and only good things would occur. The issue of signing myself out of the hospital was still a hot topic. I reassured them all, I would not. Details were coming together and I knew I would be heading home soon.

The warehousing method continued. I tried my best to stay calm and not fall off the deep end. My family all knew the only way the state hospital would release me would be to another hospital. The family all gathered at Brother Tom's house to decide what hospital to move me to. Dad got a clue from his Alcoholic Anonymous and recovery friends about Mercywood Hospital in Ann Arbor that had a tremendous record. All agreed this would be the place for me. Without much difficulty the paperwork and admission process to Mercywood began.

Chapter Forty-Four

Salvation at Murcywood

This is good, and it pleasing in the sight of God our Savior, who desires all people to be saved and to come to the knowledge of the truth.
— 1 Timothy 2:3–4 EVS

I felt a very strong closeness with staff and fellow patients. I shared every patients fear—being a patient in a state hospital. Our paths had crossed through fate and the ties of togetherness would now be split. I left Traverse City State Hospital the way I came, with very little, and feeling broken. Dad and oldest brother, Bryce, drove to Traverse City Hospital with all necessary paperwork for my transfer, and assured my delivery directly to Mercywood Hospital. Responsibility of me became Dad and Bryce's mission. We loaded into Dad's favorite car, his Mercury Grand Marquis. I had the backseat to myself. I could sense how uncomfortable they were. They worried about how I would act and what would they do if I did acted up, all legitimate concerns. I let them know that after all I had been through, all I wanted was to feel the love and comfort from them and the freedom of the back seat. Our conversation was light-hearted and relaxed. They filled me in on Mercywood Hospital as one of the oldest and best psychiatric hospitals in the state run by the Sisters of

Mercy. My thoughts were on extremes, and thankfully I would be heading to the extreme side of good.

It was dark when we arrived at Mercywood a rural setting. The staff was ready for my arrival. Signing the necessary paperwork, I checked in with a few personal things. Dad gave me a few bucks in case I needed something. Thanking them both with handshakes and hugs we parted ways. They promised to be back to visit soon. My nurse showed me to my room, explaining I would be moved to a ground floor in the morning.

The old-style design with tall ceilings, leather chair, desk, and bed with thick mattress and pillow amazed me all looked so comfortable. I felt like royalty.

I had no problem falling asleep even in my manic state. The morning brought another discovery; my own private bathroom with shower, sink, and toilet. Now convinced I must be royalty my first item of business was taking a long hot shower and a nice close shave. Then I slipped into clothes Connie packed for me that Dad and Bryce delivered. Thoughts of feeling normal filled my psyche. I do feel human again.

Food was on my mind. Once again the little old ladies were behind the steam table ready to dish out whatever you desired, it was superb and no limits. This became my new Ritz Carlton of psychiatric hospital dining.

Founded in 1923, Mercywood worked to humanely treat the mentally ill. It was one of the first psychiatric hospitals in Michigan that truly treated the mentally ill. Prior to this, treatment consisted of confinement, warehousing in cells while chained like wild animals. The Sisters of Mercy Catholic nuns opened Mercywood with determination to treat mental patients with compassion, love and grace, guided by the Holy Spirit. Their goals are the same to this day.

As promised, I was transferred to ground floor that morning. Almost every patient starts at ground. Ground is the evaluation area. The length of stay is regulated by evaluation from the staff. Some patients only stay a few days and others like me stay weeks. As with most psych wards, the day-room was the focal point of my world. The locked environment played with my psyche over time. I knew the ropes, or so I thought, and in time I would be moving to the upper floors and on my way home.

Even in the confined space I used my upbeat nature to help me cope. Every morning I was always up early getting the weather report from the radio. Then I would write it down on a chalk-board in the dayroom so people could see what kind of day outside it was going to be. I did enjoy my self-appointed position, giving me a small connection to the bigger world. I hung out with fellow patients and had very interesting conversations in the dayroom.

One of my most frustrating times on ground level was nap time. Every day from 1:00 to 2:00 p.m., all patients must go to their rooms for quiet time. Being in a manic state and hardly sleeping much at all, this created an annoyance. After much negotiation with staff I was allowed to remain awake. I could leave my room and walk, but no talking, no noise. It did not take long to feel the boredom of this privilege, so I invented a game. With my back to the wall on one end of the hall I began to walk and count my steps to the other end. After a few trips I began the challenge. Walking with my eyes closed from one end, I counted my steps trying to get as close to the other end of the hall as I could. Many senses came into play, like balance, length of steps, pace. I enjoyed my new game and most of all, it met the conditions the nurses had set.

While on my walk one day, I was approached by Dr. Hemachandra filling in for my regular doctor, Dr. Vachher. He questioned my actions and asked me what I was doing. I replied, "I'm exercising my mind," and continued my routine. I was informed weeks later Dr. Hemachandra noted in my file and added to my diagnoses manic depression with schizophrenic tendencies. Medicine at its finest. This is what mentally ill people deal with throughout their whole life within the medical community. It needs to be fixed.

His observation could not have been further from the truth but everyone has an opinion. I laughed. How else you can survive?

As my days on the ground level continued I watched patients come and go. My easy-going attitude became weary. Having family visits helped ease the agony. Thoughts of Traverse City entered my mind. The injustice, the pain both clouded my reasoning. Knowing how violated I had been, left me with a loss of pleasurable feelings. The fight with police, locked in jail and experiencing the state hospital scared my gentle thoughts. I knew that if I was to leave this floor I had to have my thoughts in control, if not I could be here a lot longer.

I guess the biggest issue about being stuck on ground was there didn't seem to be a set of requirements for me to follow that would help me advance. This low point became my strength. Two words, "control" and "patience," will get me through. I can never lose touch with those words. Every morning I wake with the thought that this will be my day out, and if not I have tomorrow.

In the dayroom the local Ann Arbor radio station played. One morning I heard a song that really affected me. The musical sound of a helicopter in the background and the voice of the singer Bruce Coburn's harsh and deliberate delivery fit my mood. The song received a lot of airtime and I listened for its every play. The singer's rough voice fit my feelings perfectly. Finally, I identified the song, "If I Had a Rocket Launcher." This song helped relieve my stress in the safest way to release anger in the confines of a psychiatric hospital.

Pam, one of the nurses on ground was exceptional. She was always dressed to the nines and carried herself well with a professional and sincere attitude. She knew of my manic problem and lack of sleep. She introduced me to some new techniques in relaxation through music. She referred me to Stephen Halpern and his album *Starborn Suite* and the song "Dawn." She also told me where I could purchase music in Ann Arbor. I was touched by Pam's concern for me, and her kindness on a somewhat personal level. At Mercywood care surrounded me, whether or not I was aware of it.

Late nights were always a concern for me since I couldn't sleep. The midnight shift staff were my friends. Once they knew I was harmless and no threat, I developed a great relationship with them. As I was quiet and not disruptive I talked with Ruth for many hours, covering everything from her family, to my family, our childhoods, old friends and current events. Ruth was an aide with many years of experience and service. And she had a vision and could get my mind going in directions I never knew before. Her knowledge went far beyond books and degrees. She was the real deal. Her education consisted of life in its real form, not sugar coated. She was always willing to give of herself and ask nothing in return. Friendly, good conversation was what she produced. Talking with Ruth allowed me to think like I was a million miles from Mercywood, like sitting in the library at the University of Michigan. I was free of mental illness and living a normal life. Hope with Ruth was abundant.

Again, the common thread in my recovery from manic depression came from common people with a huge compassion for the human race, by changing and opening my mind to a relevant way of life. Not to be belittling the psychiatric establishment with all the medications and therapies, but my recovery began in a little corner of the dayroom, at the foot of my bed, or anywhere two people could converse openly. Finding truth and love, that's where I discovered my therapy.

The day finally came for Dr. Vochher to sign my transfer to level one. I was grateful because I didn't know how much longer I could have lasted on ground. My transfer was to the older part of the hospital and that's what I was hoping for. Being able to walk the hallway whenever and even sign out for a walk outside felt so great. Those little things mean so much when they have been taken from you. We called the walking track out front of the hospital designed in the shape of a heart, the "fruit loop." It was a great area for patients to release tension and to unwind; it got lots of use.

Mercywood invoked such appeal, comfort, character and peace for me. Living in the original building created visions of its past. The groundbreaking techniques implemented by the Sisters of Mercy from the beginning surely created excitement for them and some controversy within the medical community of the time.

On one of my morning walks away from the fruit loop I discovered a walkway. Coming down from the front porch was the old entrance to the original hospital. I followed the sidewalk all the way to the road in front where I found the remnants of the steel entrance gate to the grounds. In years gone by people entered though this main entrance into the asylum. I wondered how things would have been then. How different and what a refuge this would be for the ones lucky to gain entrance. My emotions were in high gear.

I those days the importance of good nutrition and mental health was not firmly linked. Today, professionals conclude that good nutrition is a big part of good mental health. The cafeteria was located in the new part of the building and once again this place was a mecca for lovers of fine food, like me. The ladies whose job it was to prepare and distribute our meals were awesome. Every meal was presented with such love and care. The taste was of the highest quality.

Personally I have learned that nutrition and good mental health complement each other, not only nutritionally but emotionally. Good food helps us feel good. The ladies of the kitchen at Mercywood were masters, presenting each meal with love and care. God bless them.

My upgrade to level one added more regimen to my life. Accepting the staff's assignments, working with my hands and thinking out problems worked well for me even in an elevated state of mania. The classes and projects at Mercywood seemed to be at a higher level. Both challenging in preparation and rewarding in completion. It created a sense of accomplishment. In level one I got along with everyone. I tried to be as helpful as possible with staff. Life was coming around and I felt some control. I had sessions with Dr. Vachher three times a week as an inpatient. Though we did disagree on some things, I felt we were making progress. One good thing about the doctor his office was only three miles from our house in Livonia making my eventual outpatient visits easy.

My recovery since leaving ground has been phenomenal and talk of my release was in the air. One thing that Dr. Vachher and I did disagree on was his assessment of me as an alcoholic. He was sure I was and I was sure I wasn't. I lived with two alcoholics, my dad and brother Tom, and countless others when I worked as a bartender. Although I did drink, it did not alienate my life. The doctor called the shots and I followed. Before I would be released he wanted me on Antabuse, a drug designed to prevent users from drinking alcohol. Drinking while on Antabuse will cause severe sickness, possible death, that simple. I started that day on Antabuse knowing that it would not be an issue for me. But also knowing I had plenty of other issues.

I had never felt so upbeat and positive about my illness before. This time I would turn the corner and make my mark. Everything seemed in control. My life became filled with little messages, signs. Something new entered my mind. I had decided to change from coffee to tea for my morning drink. No special reason just something different. The tea that the hospital provided was Salada. In making my first cups of tea, I noticed on the tea bag handle a little saying like, "How true it is unspoken anger is never regretted," and "Everybody loves a good listener," or "It often takes an important man to act unimportant." I just loved these sayings and a great way to start my day. I also added one of these quotes every day to my weather report on the blackboard—something to think about and maybe add a good thought to counteract bad ones.

One of my most favorite places in the hospital the gift shop, was operated by my favorite, Sister Mary Visitation, one of the sweetest people to ever walk this earth. She knew everything about the shop; did all the ordering and always seemed to have just the right thing at the right price for a patient's needs. Sister Mary Visitation made things happen. Although her shop was small, she was able to arrange things in such a way to have something for everyone. I kept my notes throughout my hospital stays in a blue book purchased there. I also purchased two small medals inscribed with "I am a Lutheran," a small cross, and a St. Dymphna medal.

The care and attention directed to the mentally ill at Mercywood is beyond belief. They surrounded one with positive reinforcement and constant involvement in a clever way. The love surrounded me. The place dearest to my heart was the small chapel, seating maybe forty. It contained beautiful stained glass windows on either side, portraying Bible stories. Some of my closest moments with God took place in that chapel. The doors were always open. I could enter, sit and pray or just feel the spirit.

The Pastor in charge at Mercywood a wonderful person and a Lutheran minister, operated the chapel in a Catholic hospital. Pastor Don Niswinder and I quickly grew a friendship that helped me through a very rough time with my faith, losing it and yearning to recover it. He was a small man in stature, about five feet four inches, but his heart and soul were immeasurable.

He and his family spent seven years in Japan as missionaries a time very dear to them, before coming to Mercywood. He talked about their experiences with me. Having my faith, then losing it and now longing to again get close to Jesus, Pastor Don was an angel from heaven. We met in the chapel many times for long discussions. He always made communion available for me, no questions asked. I received the sacraments often in that little Catholic chapel from a Lutheran Pastor. God is good.

St. Dymphna is recognized in the Catholic faith today as the patroness of those who suffer from mental illness. Her feast day is May 15. The crown of martyrdom was bestowed upon her about the year 1620 and is a very visible icon at Mercywood.

One treatment for mental illness, which I never experienced, but observed patients who did, is electroshock therapy (ECT). It was discussed in my case. However I was responding to medication during my treatment. The people I did know that received the treatments showed remarkable improvements. The treatment consisted of mild sedation and then electric impulses sent through the brain. Each treatment lasted about an hour and was done three times a week. The people I observed in treatment felt the results was impressive. People who were so depressed and not communicating came out of the session with noticeable change, looking more alert and even talking. This was a very controversial treatment with very positive results.

Fred was a patient who made a lasting impact on me. He carried himself well, always dressed smart and I could tell he was a well-educated man, an engineer by trade. He attempted suicide, his reason for being a patient at Mercywood. Fred and I talked many hours in the day room about many different subjects. Of all the patients I was acquainted with he was the most enjoyable and most puzzling. I could not figure in my mind why he was there; he did not fit in. This is a chilling example of how indiscriminate mental illness is, with its ability to arise and make a connection to anyone, anytime. There are no molds, anyone can fit. Is this a reason mental illness carries such a negative perception?

One day I expressed to Fred my misunderstanding of electricity and he offered his basic explanation to help me out. His example used a piece of hose with water running through it freely. Then a child puts a stone in the hose restricting the flow; this is "ohms," a measure of resistance. What pushed the water through is "volts." The amount of water flowing through the hose is "current." E = IR only in DC. This was Fred's answer to my question, I'm not sure if it's correct or not, but it sure sounded good.

My recovery progressed. Manic thoughts that controlled me subsided. No longer were my racing thoughts controlling me; things were slowing down. My grandiose thoughts of being so smart and a know it-all, changed. How this was happening is only a guess. Correct medications played a part in this change. Human interactions with patients and staff helped me view things differently. And the one thing with no physical involvement that influenced me the most, was faith. Guiding my soul at Mercywood, with the Catholic faith influence and Pastor Don with his personality, made a compelling impact on my behavior. Time alone in my room, having a one-on-one with myself and vanishing to the bowels of my mind were the thoughts and actions that drove me to become completely fed-up with the illness. I wanted it to disappear so badly, and I would do whatever I could to control it instead of it controlling me. Once again I made a promise to myself. I was going to overcome its grip on me and would accept nothing less.

I felt progress in putting my life together. Mercywood exposed patients to the complete package of moral support and patient interaction, along with interesting and informative classes, openness of faith and religion, staff involvement and interaction, and a true sense of caring.

Patients laughed at most therapy classes. Classes were well organized and equipped with excellent supplies and were designed to challenge the patient's abilities. When implemented, both physical and mental senses were utilized and improved. The best part was when patients completed a nice piece and felt a sense of individual accomplishment. Other classes like "group therapy" allowed true thoughts and expressions of real feelings. Then patients experienced someone else's viewpoints and had the ability to incorporate these statements into their own life. Patients desperately looking for answers may find a path they had never been on that fits their issues, adding new ideas or prospects. This also helped patients realize they were not alone; other people think and feel similarly. This seems so simple and it is.

Chapter Forty-Five

Last Trip to Murcywood

The mind is like the stomach. It's not how much you
put into it that counts, but how much it digests.
— E. C. Mckenzie, *Quips and Quotes*

Adding all my time (almost two months) from jail, the state hospital in Traverse City and Mercywood, I have been on a long journey. Home was sounding mighty good, a place distant and so dear to my heart. I know that I have made good progress since coming to Mercywood, but who knows the key to open the door to freedom. The way the staff interacted with me and my sessions with Dr. Vochher, told me my departure was getting near. During my next session with the doctor, while Connie was present, an agreement was reached, I was to be released to home under her watchful eye. It was a strange feeling at first, with memories of departing months ago. I felt uncomfortable in my own home.

That dreadful day finally came for me, the day that was hidden in the back of my mind during this whole tribulation. It surfaced when Connie told me she filed for divorce, explaining this was not because she did not love me, but because she could not stand by and watch me self-destruct. It just became too much to manage for her. With all the upheaval in my life I somewhat understood her position.

This woman was dragged through hell by me and was always there. With all the fear, disappointment, unknowns, she maintained and persevered, she did it all: a full-time job, raising an eight year-old daughter, paying the bills and running our household. While confined to a mental hospital carrying that load, she still made time to visit me. No normal woman would bargain for this and rightly so, but Connie did. If there was a medal of honor for wives she should be wearing it. Super human acts beyond normal human capabilities; this type of love has no measure.

Still I would not agree for the divorce to occur easily. I was ready to fight and fight like never before, as long as I knew she still loved me. I would carry on to save my marriage to my junior high sweetheart. At home a few weeks later I was served papers for this coldhearted act. This motivated me immeasurably. I wanted to show Connie that I was still the same guy she went steady with in school and walked with down the aisle. This is just a side road, a detour in life. We will get back together on the road of life stronger and healthier than ever. My mission appeared very clearly now.

Although I still had complications adjusting to medications, lack of self-confidence, and loneliness I pursued my mission. Spending time praying, reading, doing small home repair projects and trying to set some course of action. It was all I had and I would make the most of it. Other than being served papers, life at home became quite normal. I knew as long as Connie loved me, I could overcome anything. My purpose was to prove to her I was everything I always was and even more. It is believed there is a trigger that sends one into a manic/depressed event. I also believe there is a trigger to send one out of a manic/depressed faze, and this was my trigger.

It always happens that just when things are going smoothly and life is showing signs of normalcy that manic depression rears its ugly head. At this point I considered myself a veteran in this war and survived some horrific battles. My battle with police, locked in jail, having delusional thoughts on a regular basis. Knowing fact from fiction was disorienting. With experience comes knowledge. Feelings of grandiose ideas and rapid judgments were flowing through my brain. I knew what was coming. I wanted to handle this on my own and not disrupt the family, hoping that this episode to be mild and not traumatic. I wanted to be proactive and show that I could manage my life.

I drove myself to Mercywood and entered the admissions office. I knew my only hope was there. If a solution was to be found, it would be at Mercywood. I had nowhere else to turn, this was my last hope for help. Any other stop would be a tragedy. This was a staggering feeling. In the process of being admitted I was informed that Dr. Vachher no longer worked at the hospital. He had moved from the area. For that reason I could not be admitted without a doctor. So I asked nicely to please find me a doctor, I needed to be here. I waited patiently all day with the anxiety of not being admitted. I was carrying a lot of emotional baggage and the fear of what would happen if I didn't get admitted and the setback this would produce. As the day drew longer I tried to stay calm and hope for the best. Around 7:00 p.m. a nurse moved me to a room for doctor interviews.

The door finally opened and a doctor walked in and we introduced ourselves. He began questioning me. I reached into my pocket and pulled out a cigarette, but before I could get it lit the doctor stopped me and said that I could not smoke because he was allergic. I became agitated. Remembering all the hoops that I had jumped through while biting my tongue, doing whatever was needed to stay on the straight and narrow I was annoyed. I had enough.

I turned to the doctor and said if I can't smoke he would have leave. "You're fired!" He looked at me with a look of disbelief and shock and walked out. I had reached my limit. Again the staff reminded me that I would have to leave without a doctor. I asked them politely to find me a doctor that smokes and everything would be fine.

I know that my actions seemed crazy and probably were. However I had reached a point with my illness when I had to say, "Enough." I had reached my limit and couldn't take any more. This time I made a stand and held my ground. I won't jump through more hoops.

It was close to 10:00 p.m. when again I entered the interview room praying that this will be the answer to my predicament. Finally, the door opened and a tall thin man entered the room. He introduced himself as Dr. Ramirez and we exchanged a handshake. A lot can be understood about a handshake. His felt firm, giving me a positive feeling, not overbearing. We then sat down and he reached into his pocket, pulled out a pack of cigarettes and offered me one. We both lit up and began to talk. Sitting there, the two of us smoking in a hospital gave me a feeling of being privileged in a very special way. For once my desires were understood. I did have value and I did matter. As simple a move as this was, the effects were profound. It was the turn of my true recovery from this hideous disease. Dr. Ramirez and I talked for close to an hour. His questions were different. They were not just a formality going through the motions. He showed a true concern in his voice and facial expressions. This moment in time marked an epiphany, a turning point in my journey. Dr. Ramirez finished his notes and ended our first late-night session with a promise to return tomorrow and to continue our discussion, adding that he would gladly take me on as a new patient.

Now with a doctor's review, I could be admitted. The nurse on staff finished the details, adding me in the ground floor, the place where almost all patients start at Mercywood. I knew the routine and was ready to make progress in removing this ball and chain I had been dragging around for way too long. I easily fell into the routine on ground. It felt like my second home by now.

I moved up from ground within four days to level one, mainly because I had been a patient before. They knew my history and I showed no real concerning signs. The routine and freedom of level one worked out well.

I almost never remember my dreams while sleeping, however I have had delusional thoughts. One started in my mind. The scene that played out was that I had some special "secret" information planted on me by Russian spies and now they wanted it back. These thoughts started slowly and built. I never mentioned this to staff thinking I could handle it and they would go away. These thoughts and visions were as real as the nose on my face. I could not differentiate these thoughts from any other thoughts in my mind.

While sitting in occupational therapy class working on my project a strong perception overcame me that the Russians were close by and wanted to take back whatever I had of theirs. I felt I was being watched from all directions. I imagined that what they wanted I had in my clothing. As the anxiety and fear grew, and the feeling that they were moving in on me, I felt the need to escape.

I jumped from the table, ran to the door and down the hall while peeling off my clothes, hoping to remove the secret package I was carrying. Just about the time I had my clothes off the staff caught up with me. By this point my thinking became very delusional. The staff wanted to calm me down. They started injecting medications. Nothing seemed to slow me down. I was still out of control. A group of male attendants helped me in to a room on ground floor with all padded surfaces, better known as the rubber room. This is a confined area where I could not hurt myself. I was still extremely psychotic. The only thing in the room was a single mattress laying on the floor.

A small window at the top of the wall exposed the ground level outside. As the aides left I feared the thought of being locked in this room. To my relief the door was closed, but not locked. But now my demon thoughts truly overcame me. Through the small window I spotted a man standing on the sidewalk not far from me. He was sent to be my assassin. With only my briefs on I searched for their secret package and found none. Therefore, it must be planted in me. Their plan was that if they couldn't have it, they would make sure no one else would. Knowing that this was the end of line I tried to position myself in the room where my shooter wouldn't have a clean shot at me. I grabbed the mattress and positioned it in front of me, knowing this was no protection but added some comfort.

As I lay there alone I began sweating profusely. Then came the tremors. It felt like every muscle in my body was in an uncontrollable spasm. Convinced that at any time a bullet would be coming through the window ending my life, I prayed for God to protect me.

In an instance an encounter like no other feeling I had ever known, and no words can describe, this absolute calm overcame me. A voice said, "Everything will be okay, do to fear." The sweating and shakes ceased. And then the most peaceful feeling saturated my body like nothing I had experienced in this world. Now lying on the mattress completely tranquil, I drifted off to sleep. When I awoke I spotted the most unusual sight. Sitting in a chair in my room was Ruth II, the aide from the midnight shift on one-west. This was the person I enjoyed many great discussions with and truly appreciated her company. I looked at her with a perplexed face and asked why she was there. With a calm reassuring look, she said because she heard I was having a rough time and she just wanted to come and sit with me.

She exhibited to me one of the greatest selfless acts of kindness a person can give to another. She adjusted her times to be with me. Even in a psychotic, heavily drugged state Ruth II touched me deep inside. Her actions smashed the wall between my mental illness and normal thinking. Ruth demonstrated to me that day the true feeling of unconditional love. Don't tell me there are no angels among us.

Although I was delusional and psychotic every thought in my life at that moment was very real. In my mind, it was all legitimate, reality and fantasy became the same with absolutely no difference.

Clinicians tell me this episode was merely the effects of the strong medications administered to me. I say hogwash! Only one factor carried me through that fear, raging in my mind and body. That was the power of Christ's love. Meds may have assisted me falling off to sleep, however, the spirit of Jesus Christ controlled entirely the whole event.

Because of this incident I was sent back to ground for just a few days as a precaution. The incident was not down played or up played by staff, it just was. It wasn't long before I was back in my old room on level one. I spent time with Dr. Ramirez making some real progress. This man really touched my heart. He showed very little concern about my past episode. He based my therapy on my future and things that could be accomplished rather than letting this illness anchor me down. This caused me to believe I am somebody of value. This was not the normal plan or procedure of other psychiatrists I had dealt with. I felt that others just wanted me to take my meds, lay low, think simple thoughts and not make waves, and see them on a regular basis.

I got back into the daily routine by going to classes, visiting the gift shop for little things and chatting with Sister Mary Visitation. I spent a lot of time in the day room with other patients resolving all the world problems. It was peaceful.

As with all groups there is always one who rubs everyone wrong. Ours was Marcellus, a man who just could not shut up and had an answer for everything. His personality was known by everybody including the staff. The problem was that everyone tolerated his behavior. This bothered me. He always seemed to sit in the most comfortable chair. We listened daily to his rants. One of them was about his time as a soldier in the Vietnam War. He went on and on about his heroic deeds while in country.

Though I did not serve in Vietnam I had friends who did and I learned many stories of battles and heroism from them. One friend did not return, making the ultimate sacrifice. My friends spoke the truth. Strangely enough, Marcelles stories were different slanted so he was the hero. My hero friends conveyed a completely different story, because it was often very hard to express their emotions and feelings while speaking from the heart. Not Marcellus. His tales were like a John Wayne movie and he was John Wayne.

After listening the better part of the morning to John Wayne, I had had enough. My blood was boiling. I could not listen any more. I jumped up from my chair and climbed on his chair with my knees on his thighs and my hands on his shoulders. I shouted to him, "You're full of crap! Liar! If it does not stop, I will stop it for you." It wasn't long before staff removed me from atop him. Once again I was escorted back to ground. This time things were somewhat different. Everyone knew why I was in ground and everyone supported me. Staff and patients alike were all happy someone called down Marcelles. Everyone had had their fill of him. My punishment was minimal. He apparently told everyone that he would sue me, the hospital, and the doctors. It made me feel good that everyone supported me and I was not alone. Nothing ever came of the incident.

In a very positive way my sessions continued with Dr. Ramirez and the day-to-day life continued routinely. Long days in the day room contemplating the world's problems with fellow patients helped ease the boredom. My stay this time was approaching twenty-two days and rumors were floating about my departure. I felt my head was more together than at any time in the past four years. I had a real desire to make something happen with my life. While I was sitting in the day room one day a patient came over to me. I do not remember his name, but I will never forget his face. We had spent some time together and our thoughts were on the same page. Sitting next to me he pulled out a cross on a chain and begin to fiddle with it. He said he wanted to give it to me as a gift. I was humbled by his gesture of kindness. He was a patient who I did have pleasant talks with on faith and religion. I watched as he took the ring from the top of the cross where the chain goes through, removing the ring using only his fingers. I was amazed with his strength and ability. This was not easy even with tools. He turned and handed me only the cross. My thought was that he did not want me to wear it as a necklace but carry it in my pocket or display it. I have it to this day. Somehow it ended up on my tool bench in my garage. Why is it there? I don't know but I do know this, I see it on a regular basis and think of the day it's was given to me. It's is a good spot for it.

The day came for my departure and Connie was there. The last thing was the exit review with Dr. Ramirez. The three of us entered a small office near the nurse's station. Dr. Ramirez began to review my progress. He then disclosed the most profound statement I have ever heard from a psychiatrist. He stated that if I stayed on my meds, observed my actions through my wife's eyes, letting her be the lead to judge my condition, and continued my current lifestyle there was a good chance that I would never have to be in another psychiatric hospital again. Or maybe only for a slight medication adjustment. I was blown away by this statement. I thought I would be in and out of these places for the rest of my life. Those words did so much for my self-confidence. I could be a normal person and live a normal life. No doctor ever talked to me like that. I was on cloud nine. Leaving the hospital I could not have been more pleased. Life appeared good and I was ready.

Chapter Forty-Six

Struggle Back to Normalcy

The purposes of a man's heart are deep waters, but a man of understanding draws them out.
—Proverbs 20:5 NIV

Jack Boland, a pastor with the Church of Today, entered my life. Jack held a TV service on Sunday mornings. His messages felt like they were sent directly to me. His voice was so soothing whether in prayer or reading his lesson. He told his story to anyone that was willing to listen. In his past he was a drunk living in the ghettos. The Lord lifted him and gifted him as a pastor. His first church was in Detroit. Soon a brand new church was built in Warren, Michigan. People came from all around town to hear and to be with Jack. He was a magical person, witty and always uplifting people. Within his church there were ten self-help groups. I would listen every Sunday and with a small donation a tape would be sent to my home. He was my connection with the Lord then, and it worked. I developed a deep inner peace and connection with Jesus. Jack had guest speakers, mostly well-known people. I still have some of the cassettes. Sadly Jack left us too early (cancer). He was the only person that I knew who attended his own funeral. You are missed Jack.

Life at home became comfortable without difficulty. Everyone was doing their thing—Laura at school and hanging out with friends, Connie at work. She liked her job and didn't mind going to work. The only thing lacking for me was work. I knew I needed to work and I wanted to work. Only I had no job to go to. My thoughts were occupied with memories of the past, the good times, flying, my love and getting paid to do it. Taking family camping trips with friends, being a "normal" family, together without a lot of cash, but lots of closeness. I listened to Jack Boland's tapes and read from the bible. I knew these times are in the past and must look to the future. I believed I could build a new life for us and somehow I was going to get there.

And then things changed and my prayers were answered. After a month of staying at home with only my thoughts, my dear old friend Steve Demeter stopped by the house to see how I was doing. He then asked if I would like to go to work in his garage at his house doing body work. Steve worked full time at a Ford dealer body shop and was one of the top techs in the business. Steve had always kept his clientele from the days of S&J Collision. This was where Steve and John Watterson educated me in the business, while I attended flight school.

Steve made me an offer to work for him that was almost too good to be true. It was a perfect fit, working the hours I wanted. If I did not feel good, I could just stay home. I would be working on my own with direction from Steve. He would give me my assignments in the evening for the following day. I couldn't pass up this opportunity. It was just the job I needed at this point in my life.

I was a working man with someplace to go to use my mind and body. Steve told me to keep track of my hours and he would pay me cash on Fridays. I was excited knowing that I would have challenges. It had been a sufficient amount of time since I done this work and not having someone to bounce questions off was challenging. But I could call Steve if I had a question or problem.

Off I went. Most of the jobs Steve took on in the garage were not hard hits, mainly fender benders. It took some time but I was back at it. Steve was the final inspector and if a panel needed a little extra work he would help me. Steve did all the final paintwork. Our system worked and I had cash coming in.

This was the perfect job for me at this point in my life. And life was becoming more normal. I think Steve knew what an effect his offer played in my life and if he forgot, I reminded him. And I was not the only one he helped. He responded to many people's hardships. Steve is another guardian angel in my life.

Our daughter was graduating from high school in June and Connie and I wanted to do something nice for her. Time as a parent seemed to pass me by, I did my best and my love never wavered. Laura was a good kid with a great personality, well adjusted, considering the conditions. She grew up fast. We came to the conclusion that a car would be a nice gift. With limited funds we began our search for an affordable car. It wasn't long before we spotted a nice red 1978 Mustang, owned by an older gentleman. It looked solid, like something I could work with. We bought it and I took it to Steve's shop. Knowing space was at a premium there I had to work fast. I started the body work after hours and on weekends. Overall the body was in good shape with no rust, just some dents. I purchased a new complete carpet for it knowing that would make a great improvement in the overall look. The mechanical side was good. I had it checked out. I decided to paint the body myself. My first complete paint job surprisingly turned out splendid.

A party was planned at the clubhouse at my mom's condo. Towards the end everyone gathered in the parking lot. Sitting there was the red Mustang with a big bow on it. Laura was stunned and taken by surprise. It was a good day. The irony of the story was that after about a year Laura came to me and asked if I would be hurt if she sold the Mustang. I hold her it was her car and she could do whatever she wanted, I wouldn't feel hurt. She sold it and bought a Honda.

As usual, life never stays the same. Steve told me of a job at Plymouth Auto Body, a shop he started years ago. The current owner John Miller, was looking for someone to manage and work in the shop. Steve really urged me to take this job, assuring me that I was ready for it. I thought long and hard. Was I ready? Could I confront the public? Do I have the inner strength to overcome whatever thoughts will challenge me? I chose to give it an attempt.

I made an appointment to meet with the owner to get more details. After our meeting I liked what he had to say and felt it was something I could manage. Learning the management side could be beneficial to me. I decided to make the move. Steve gave me his blessing and with a bucket full of encouragement, off I went. This job was a boost in pay which always makes things brighter.

As soon as I arrived at Plymouth Auto Body, the owner, John, departed, leaving me a phone number if I had questions. There was only one other employee in the shop, a young man with not a lot of experience. The two of us held down the fort. I was spending a lot of time in the office with all the duties necessary to run the shop. I would rather be in the shop, but the office duties kept me away. Things were going okay and we were keeping the doors open. I began to really enjoy working with the customers and insurance companies and felt I had a knack for it with my personality and gift of gab. I also was learning a lot of new skills.

It was at this time Connie and I needed to talk. The subject was divorce papers. We talked about my understanding and growth with the illness. My stable life-style gave me a true desire to keep our marriage together. All things considered, Connie felt secure with me and my illness. We were still in love with each other. Seeing a brighter future she rescinded the divorce proceedings. I could not have been happier. Connie was still the love of my life, adding more good things into my life and giving me a second chance. I was blessed.

Once again fate soared into the picture. John came to the shop to tell me that he had some buyers that sounded very interested. A few days later they came to look the place over. They liked it. The deal closed fast. John was happy, but not me. The new owners would not need me. They would be handling everything themselves. It wasn't long before I was out looking for work again—not a great feeling.

Again, I found a want ad in the *Detroit News*. Someone wanted a body shop manager. I immediately called and was informed the shop was on Ford Road in Westland not far from home, a new franchise store named Kales Collision. This was new in the collision business and becoming popular. I set up a date to interview. My first contact was with the franchisee, Rick Wilson, who had no body shop experience. He worked for Oakland County, and his brother Roger was to be a silent partner. My interview went well and I think he wanted to hire me on the spot. The next day I was hired. The brand new shop was just a few weeks from opening in a nice new building with all new equipment.

With great anticipation opening day came. It was a big deal with lots of hoopla. This was the first time I met Kale, the franchise owner. I had heard he had a shaky background, but he was always pleasant to me. The business took off like gangbusters at this great location. We were busy right from the start. It was nice to just manage the shop and not have to do collision repair as well. I had my hands full with all the managing duties. Rick's wife, Terry, worked with me at the front desk doing paper work and greeting customers. That was okay with me. I had plenty to do writing estimates, ordering parts and dealing with the shop and insurance adjusters. Things were going great and after a few months the corporate people came in and gave me an award for the best new store start-up in Kales short history. Everyone was delighted. It put our little store on the front page. We were the place where everyone wanted to be.

It was spring of 1987. I settled into my new job dealing with customers and employees. The company family members also kept me on my toes. I was amazed how many people were drawn to our shop. I never knew if it was the name or the location, but we stayed busy. After a couple of years I was in my groove and comfortable. When corporate opened a new franchise, the franchisee ended up in our store and I was the trainer. I felt good about that. I liked working with people and helping others learn the business.

One of my trainees was Dick Henderson, a new franchisee who was eager to make his shop the best. Dick was born with a birth defect and was missing half of his right arm. This did not hold him back and he was aggressive and eager to learn. For some reason he thought the sun rose and set over me. When Dick finished his training he had a few weeks before his store would be ready. Being from the east side of Detroit (15 Mile and Mound) and close to the GM Tech Center. His shop was a little smaller than Westland, but that could be in his favor. Not long after Dick completed training I was asked to come work for him. He had a decent pay plan. My biggest hurdle was the distance. It's on the opposite side of town.

Dick persisted, and I started to think. The family life at the Westland store was getting heavy and I seemed to be in the middle of it. I always liked the challenge of a new opening. The big question is, how do I do this and not ruffle anyone's feathers. When I approached Rick, the Westland store owner of my intentions, he thought he could handle the manager job and also save some money.

I made the move to Warren, a long ride from Livonia. This was before I-696, so the only road was 8 Mile, not the most scenic route to drive, but the quickest. Dick Henderson's wife, Jeanine also worked in the office with me. The Warren store never had the energy like the Westland store. Early on the finger pointing started. I knew I could bring in customers. There were no customers coming in. This made for uneasiness and had me looking over my shoulder.

Then came a call at three in morning from Dick. There had been a fire in the shop that night and he needed me in as soon as possible. By the time I arrived the fire was out. The damage was dreadful. We had twenty-two customer cars in the shop that day. All with damage and the shop was completely covered in black soot. The scene was shocking. By morning insurance companies were arriving to assess the damage. I was informed that the shop's insurance policy allowed for one employee to be on the payroll through the repair time, this would be me. My first assignment entailed calling all the customers that had cars in the shop and inform them of the disaster. That was a tough morning. Everyone was upset and rightly so. It became one of the longest days of my life, the most stressful since rejoining the work force. At times I would walk away and take a break from it. I was dealing with a lot of pressure, however I could control the calls. Comforting customers in place of stressing them helped me to complete the task and to plan for more coming.

The damage to the vehicles varied, some were total losses, others questionable. I'm glad this would be determined by the insurance adjusters. The first people to arrive were from AAA. Their local office was close, bringing a group of adjusters to inspect the twelve vehicles they insured. To my surprise, they totaled all their vehicles. I was told that their experience taught them that in a situation like this it was best to wipe the slate clean, ending any chance for repercussions down the road. Other companies went the repair route. The amazing thing was that it took less than two months to put the shop back to its brand new condition.

Things were still not going well within the company. Dick was having second thoughts about buying the shop, realizing this is not an instant money maker and having no shop experience made it tough.

I could see the writing on the wall and I began to put out feelers. Once again the *Detroit News* classifieds came through. I noted a small ad looking for a body shop manager at Gordon Chevrolet, just a few miles from my home. I was so excited about this job. This would be my dream job, a department manager for a major dealership, one of the top jobs in the field and also in compensation.

I prayed this interview would go well. I knew that there would be stiff competition and I was ready to give it my all. I met with the general manager, Art Smith and had a good interview. I could tell he was looking for experience, but also personality. I worked at bringing across my outgoing personality and my ability to get the job done right. I knew that Art was looking for someone with great people expertise and talent, a most important skill dealing with customers.

I received a call about one week later for a second interview. I was so excited I could hardly stand it. The night of the interview I focused on being positive minded and extremely sincere. Art Smith had a few questions for me. First he asked if I would have a problem shaving my beard. (At the time I wore a well-trimmed beard.) He informed me that managers could not have beards. My response was that I can have it off tomorrow. The last question, could I start there in a week. I responded that I will make that happen. With that he welcomed me to Gordon Chevrolet. I can't explain appropriately my feelings. It was so overwhelming. I was the one picked over so many applicants. I wanted to jump up and scream with joy. I had reached the top of body shop managers' level. Now the most important issue was to produce. Art had given me an assessment of the department. Bob, the current manager was close to retirement and had just lost his wife to cancer. I was told customer care and growth would be a top priority for me. The assistant, Don, would stay on board until I was up to speed. Bob would also stay on for a month to help my transition to this job.

Now I had to break the news to Dick Henderson. I did not feel real bad about leaving. I was very excited to give up my daily drive to the east side of Detroit. When I told Dick of my plans to leave he told me he was close to selling the business, another reason I was glad to be leaving. With all said and done I packed up and never returned to 15 Mile and Mound.

Starting my new job at Gordon Chevrolet was a huge move upward for me. Harboring all the mental issues in my life, feeling ashamed and a lesser person, with all these past thoughts and feelings and not wanting them to be exposed to others, troubled me. This can never be divulged. Looking back on all the years of instability and volatility in my life with mental illness, and the insecurity of my financial position weighted heavily on my mind. In a perfect world I was accepted as I was. However, I thought of all the life experiences I could offer my counterparts and enlighten them, and maybe even improve their management abilities if my past be known. I have nothing to hide and I am not ashamed of my past but this must stay concealed. If I exposed my illness to my colleagues it would be their answer to all my shortcomings. An easy reason to justify any mistakes I made. Another example of injustice of the mentally ill.

Steve, what more can I say

Laura's red Mustang

after the shop fire

Chapter Forty-Seven

Life in Balance Accepting Manic Depression

For I will restore health to you, and your wounds I
will heal, declares the Lord, because they have called
you an out-cast: "It is Zion, for whom no one cares."
—Jeremiah 30:17 ESV

The days of cutting lawns for five dollars an hour looked like the best life had to offer me. With the help of some wonderful friends, my dear family, and a great doctor, I was able to move forward. There were so many people in my life, some long-lasting, others a mere flash that I am forever grateful to.

Dealing with my illness to help keep me in the real world and out of psychiatric hospitals, I have devised a few life plans. Accepting my situation as is, and not trying to change reality. Finding new ideas to cope and grow within the illness. Honest and open thoughts can be endless. Accepting first, opens the door of desire for change. Control, realize and act when thoughts and actions change, and are not your normal way of behaving. Exposure after diagnosis with this illness allows for self-analysis. Knowing the desire to change and improve must be paramount. Depression is a huge issue, but for me, not as terrifying as mania, thank God! Depression is a real killer and in the long term has to be tackled! In my case, depression did not rear its ugly head often. I was able to deal with it by surrounding myself with my favorite things, thoughts and people. I learned how powerful this thinking can be for me. I must confess that pharmacology in the field of depression has powerful results and many successful outcomes. And I acknowledge some of my depressions were controlled by medication. This point I cannot stress enough that pills only work if you take them as prescribed. Why patients don't feel better is mostly just for that reason. Over time, if medicine does not show results, tell your doctor and a change will be made. I have been guilty of this behavior. It's human nature but must be overcome. As for mania this moves fast. The reason Dr. Ramirez chose my wife to be the one to sound the alarm if change came to me. This technique was successful for my protection, however at times very frustrating for me. Every little change I made would be examined. "Are you okay?" repeatedly asked to the point I was going cuckoo. I played the game because I knew if I resisted it all would fall apart. I played along for my own well-being. Mania is sensuous like a drug. It allows for that euphoric feeling, a sense of you can do anything, mental or physical. Possessing super human abilities, and no one can tell you differently. My solution for this was mind control. When racing thoughts and grandiose ideas appeared, like not sleeping for days because a had so much to do I didn't have time for sleep, or drive fifty miles to a certain restaurant because they were the only place for a special type of food I craved. I would close my eyes and relax as in therapy focusing on personal good thoughts, to alter the manic ideas. I relate it to a scene from the movie *The Perfect Mind* at the end when John Nash has overcome his demons but will still see them at times. When this happens he recognizes them and turns away, wanting nothing to do with them, knowing they were evil and would lead him astray.

My biggest blessing is my faith in Jesus Christ instilled in me early on by my parents. At times this has been an on-again-off-again relationship. Again I have experienced His love and grace in my life. It was the times I was in my worst sickness that He never left me. When comfort and peace were needed He was there, always loving. I truly believe without his intervention I most likely would not have survived.

The facts are, I am here and I need to find my purpose. I survived a plane crash and mental illness. I have spent many hours searching for the answer. Why am I still here? I have pursued many people and places without a secure answer to this. Why am I still here when many people experiencing the same circumstances are not? I searched and searched for this answer to no avail. I live my life knowing that relapse is a very real possibility. This is not like cancer in remission, and the further out the odds for survival increase. It has been many years since I have had a full blown episode and I feel blessed. Why, I do not know. I can only continue to live my life as I have conditioned myself to live and if the big altercation comes, I will transition and sound the alarm.

I had no real mission when I started to write, other than friends and family said I should write a book. As this evolved, a strong desire overcame me, and the need to share thoughts and express my life's lessons became a passion to pass to anyone who has an interest. This is me and cannot be changed, even as hard at times as I have tried. This is to be my story in the fourth quarter of my life. It fits my style, to give, knowing it may have stirred something or someone in the delivery. I'm searching. I do not wish to change the world. My drive now is the fact that I no longer have to hide the painful truth of my past, as I did for so many years. Now I can say whatever I want, and I am ready to say it not as a dissident but as a peaceful survivor from my experiences in life. I don't want to waste this experience or bore people with it, but I have a strong passion to pass it on.

I was talking about the plane crash with an old pilot friend, Jeff Kilponen, a captain for Southwest Airlines. He introduced one of their pilots to me that had extensive training in crisis counseling related to aircraft incidents. After a long phone conversation and relaying to him my story, he said, "You are searching for an answer that is not there. There is no answer. Let it be and move on with your life." As simple as his words were, coming from him, it stuck. What do I do now? With all the near-death experiences in my life, I do believe the Lord loves me and does have a plan for keeping me on this earth. The only question is, for what? I am still searching and I know He will reveal it to me at the right time. Or maybe I am living that life now and don't realize it. I try to live my life with Christ's guidance, "saved" with a helpful, caring existence. Do unto others as you would have them do unto you.

There but for the grace of God go I.

This new job as a department manager for a large auto dealership offered me the spectacle of returning from a war after a long, grueling pilgrimage, as a survivor. I arrived at a place where I would be considered normal. The best way to describe this condition normal is this way. I have many friends, close and not as close, also lots of past fellow workers and acquaintances in my life. They will read this story not knowing the true story, and say, "He seemed so normal, he was so likeable, a hardworking man, and great to know." And some will be shocked, thinking, "This couldn't be the same guy." But how many will view me differently? The tasks ahead will be significant and demanding. My desire to succeed and produce a quality life to the best of my ability is my vision. I recognize this as just another journey through life, and where the next pathway will lead me, only He knows.

My girls

Connie and Jim night out

Steve Demeter and John Salvatore late night fishing trip

fun flying

me and Safu at Detroit City Airshow enjoying some R&R time

About the Author

My name is James Lowell Hawk, and I have lived almost my whole life in the great state of Michigan. I have been blessed with many life's experiences. Having compiled fourteen hospitalizations and major surgeries so far in this life and still in respectable health, I am blessed. This memoir describes mainly the first fifty years of my life on this earth. Throughout my life's encounters I have been encouraged by many people to write my story. Having been encouraged but never making time to put it to paper and overcoming my weakest points, spelling and grammar were my stumbling blocks. Finally, after retiring, the desire still there and with time to commit to the project, my journey begin. I must admit along this path I have acquired the skills and dedication of some wonderful people by chance and openly. They reaffirmed to me the true meaning of giving freely and the blessing it brings.

I was raised in the suburbs of Detroit, Michigan, during the fifties and sixties, and what a time it was. WWII was won, subdivisions were going up everywhere, schools were full, dads worked and moms were moms, and everyone had time and money for summer vacations. Little League sports, scouting, and church were family events. As kids, we always hung out together doing anything and everything together as a group. We developed camaraderie learning to watch each other's backs even in disputes (and there were many); we bonded. We were our own entertainment, no iPads then. In this environment we learned compassion, commitment, and unity.

I am proud to say, to this day a handful of those friends from back then are still in my life, and we communicate on a regular basis. We have lost a few along the way. My prayer is we will all be together in eternity with our heavenly Father.